EVOLVE AND CONQUER

A Collection Of Stories From Entrepreneurs On Their Greatest Moments Of Change

Queens In Business & Inspired By

EVOLVE AND CONQUER
A Collection Of Stories From Entrepreneurs On Their Greatest Moments Of Change

ISBN: 9781068728204 Paperback

Published By: Inspired By Publishing

Cover Designed By: Tanya Grant - The TNG Designs Group Limited

The strategies in this book are presented primarily for enjoyment and educational purposes. Every effort has been made to trace copyright holders and obtain their permission for the use of copyright material.

The information and resources provided in this book are based upon the authors' personal experiences. Any outcome, income statements or other results, are based on the authors' experiences and there is no guarantee that your experience will be the same. There is an inherent risk in any business enterprise or activity and there is no guarantee that you will have similar results as the author as a result of reading this book.

The author reserves the right to make changes and assumes no responsibility or liability whatsoever on behalf of any purchaser or reader of these materials.

Acknowledgements

By Chloë Bisson

Founder of Inspired By Publishing

I believe that inspiring others is one of the most beautiful gifts that we give to others during our lifetimes. Whether it's inspiring our friends, our families, our children, our clients or even ourselves at times.

That's why I want to give a special thank you to each of the collaborators who opened up and shared their stories within these pages with the view to inspire you, our reader. The dedication and commitment to be part of a project like this doesn't go unnoticed so thank you for coming on the journey with us and trusting us to share your story with the world.

I want to also give a special thank you to our dedicated publishing team at Inspired By Publishing whose talent and commitment made this book possible. To Sunna Coleman for managing and inspiring our team and to Angela Haynes-Ranger and Gaby Osias for your incredible eye for detail and editing skills. To Tanya Grant whose beautiful designs bring this book to life, and to Alex Padua for making sure this book gets published and into your hands.

Finally, I want to give an extra special thank you to Shim Ravalia, Sunna Coleman and Tanya Grant for being the leaders of this collaborative book series. Without you, this book series would merely be a dream. Your belief in our joint mission to empower and inspire others through our books has been unwavering and so thank you for everything.

Dedication

We dedicate this book to all those who brave leaving their comfort zone to enhance not only their life but the lives of those around them.

Table of Contents

Introduction 1

Change Is Inevitable - Chloe Bisson 3

Never Knew Me Until You - Sunna Coleman 19

Entrepreneurship Is An Inside Job - Shim Ravalia 34

All In the Name Of Change! - Tanya Grant 46

A Life By Design - Chris Hill 62

Rewiring Your Brain - Taiba Bajar 75

"What Do I Desire?" - Mart Tweedy 90

The Joy Of Collecting Experience - Annette Corbett 106

Transforming Trauma Into Triumph - Dan Todd 125

From Developing Websites To
Developing People - David Thorne 141

Fear To Success To Fear Again - Andy Nisevic 158

Adapt To Change - Rebecca Tsang Mang Kin 174

Navigating Change - Suzette Metz 195

Conclusion 210

Introduction

There's no denying that life is unpredictable, and more often than not, we're compelled to make changes we hadn't prepared for or anticipated. Many of us find ourselves in challenging situations that force us to adapt, sometimes requiring us to change aspects of our lives or ourselves that we weren't quite ready to change.

Change can be daunting, especially for those who crave stability and clarity. It forces us to confront fears and insecurities that we often shy away from, yet embracing change is essential for embracing life itself. To navigate life's unpredictability, learning how to adapt to new conditions becomes crucial in dealing with the twists and turns of fate.

There are moments when we look back and connect the dots, understanding why certain changes were necessary. After all, life is a continuous journey of moving forward and evolving. Each change we go through signifies growth and a desire for better things. It allows our world to broaden, embracing newness and endless aspirations.

In this book you will find the incredible stories of entrepreneurs who have gone through significant changes in their lives. It was a journey of letting go, unlearning, and embracing renewal and transformation simultaneously. Through their experiences, they have emerged as inspirational leaders, mastering the art of adjusting to change and shedding old limitations that once held them back.

These are individuals who have bravely welcomed change, allowing them to become the person they always aspired to be.

Change Is Inevitable

Chloë Bisson
Two Time #1 Bestselling Author, Award Winning Speaker & Founder
Inspired By Publishing

"Change Is Inevitable. Growth Is Optional."– John C. Maxwell

As you're reading this book, you're probably reading some incredibly inspiring stories of change.

Change can show up in so many different ways.

Maybe you've experienced change in your career, your relationships, your health or even, your own mindset. Change is everywhere and it is the most common thing that we go through in life. It truly is one of the few things in this world that is guaranteed and inevitable, yet so many of us fight it.

So many of us try and avoid change. Most people find change uncomfortable and so it's a natural default reaction to want to avoid it, After all, why would we want to feel uncomfortable, right?

If you think about physical change for a moment, as we have physically grown in our lives, from being a new born baby to an adult, we had to change. We had to adapt physically to be able to survive. And as I'm writing this chapter currently 14 weeks pregnant, it's hard to not notice the physical change happening in my body every single day.

But imagine if we hadn't ever grown from being an infant, how could we possibly then go on to start families of our own?

Change is inevitable, and it's needed for all of us, whether we like it or not.

For me, change has been a constant in my life for as long as I can remember.

In 2001, when I was 10 years old, my parents decided to divorce and I spent the next eight years of my life living between two homes, literally changing from one home, one parent to the other every day.

You might think this sounds exhausting and painful but to me it was my new normal and the greatest thing that happened from that upbringing was that I learned how to adapt to change very quickly and very easily, with very little pain or discomfort. Given that change is inevitable, it's a skill that I'm extremely grateful I learnt at such a young age.

Maybe you're reading this book because you've been through change recently. Maybe you've experienced a change that's left you feeling great, excited, empowered and inspired. Or maybe you've gone through a change recently that's left you feeling lost, confused, alone, scared, reminiscing on what used to be or what could have been. No matter whether it's a positive or negative, it's still triggered by change.

The difference between people that thrive through change and those that struggle is their ability to understand and adapt to the change that they're experiencing.

Your ability to do this not only puts you back in the driver's seat but it also determines the outcome for the change.

For example, if you're going through a difficult change in your business, if you struggle to understand and accept it, you might find yourself fighting it and struggling through it which means the outcome is going to be less positive and the pain may even drag on for longer.

However, if you give yourself permission to understand and accept the change, no matter how long it takes, you may find yourself looking for the lessons and the positives that have come out of the change and ultimately, using that to fuel you to create an even better result than what you'd have hoped for before.

Being Open To Opportunities

It was May 2019.

I was running my own coaching business, and I was known as someone that could coach women on how to leave the corporate world and start their own business.

I'd been coaching for about three years, had started my own Facebook group, set up my own Facebook page and I had a list of paying clients who were working with me on starting their own business.

But being completely open and honest, it was really, really tough trying to grow that business. I remember that I saw so many signs that it wasn't working, but I was so adamant that I didn't want to give it up.

Despite all of the signs, I kept remembering what my friends and family said when I first started my business:

"How are you going to pay your bills?"
"What if no one wants to work with you?"
And then my age-old favourite… "When are you going to get a real job?"

Those questions played in my mind over and over and so even years into my business, whenever I thought about changing my business or changing what I did, I couldn't accept it because I felt that I would be proving those people right. I felt like I would have been seen as a failure.

So, mainly due to my ego, for years those words kept me pushing through and being too stubborn to see that my business wasn't working the way it needed to. I hustled and hustled. I read every book under the sun about how to grow a coaching business, and for some reason, it just wasn't working. Until one day, I was on a Zoom call with a potential client and it was going really well.

"It's been so great getting to know you and I feel like through the conversations that we've had, I really resonate with you and your coaching style."

All sounds good so far, right? But there was one big problem which she expressed to me very openly.

"I just can't choose between your coaching programme and other coaches that I've been researching."

Now, I'd never really looked at competitors because I'd thought all coaches were different but judging by what she was saying, the issue wasn't about my coaching programme but my authority.

She continued to tell me about other coaches whose books she'd read and podcasts she'd listen to and was asking to find out how my coaching was different to theirs. What she meant was how my coaching was better than theirs.

Despite every part of my being knowing it was the wrong thing to do, I found myself justifying why my coaching programme was better and how it was different. I knew that every word that came out of my mouth was pushing her further and further away from working with me and it just didn't feel nice at all.

Safe to say, she didn't become one of my paying clients.

At that point in my coaching business, I was completely empty. I had no more paying clients, no more enquiries from potential clients and no more money to invest in any way of getting any either. All I had left was one session with my mentor at the time and this felt like my last chance to make it work.

Even at this low point in my business, I still wasn't open to changing my business. Despite the low bank account and the bad months, I was still trying to avoid the change. I was still fighting and pushing and being so determined that I had to finish what I started and stick to what I committed to. Because ultimately, that's what entrepreneurs do, right? We push through the hard times. We have to make it work, right? After all, "winners don't quit, they keep going until they turn their failures into wins" right?

Wrong.

What I came to learn soon after is that there's a right time to walk away from something. Changing your direction doesn't mean you're a failure if change feels like the right thing to do. So back in the final mentoring session, as I was waffling on about the struggles and why I had to keep going, my mentor turned to me and said: "Chloe, there are people out there that need what you have to offer. They just don't value you enough yet."

I stopped talking and I let it sink in. After reflecting on what that meant, I started asking myself: "Well, if they don't value me enough now, how can I fix that? What can I change?"

And as soon as I started opening my mind up to change, it came to me. I looked at the other coaches that people had chosen to work with. I looked at the coaches that were doing what I wanted to do, that were speaking on stages and were known in the industry far greater than I was. And I realised they had one very big thing in common. They all had a book.

And so there and then I decided to make the first of what was going to be many changes in my business. I decided to write my first book.

I wrote my first book, Determined and Dangerous, in 10 days and I published it in 28 days. It's safe to say I wasn't wasting any more time after procrastinating and putting off the change for so long, and it was incredible.

Because I'd worked so hard on learning about marketing earlier in my business, I'd learned many different strategies on how to launch new products and how to market my business. They didn't work for the coaching services I'd been offering before but, guess what, they worked perfectly for a book. And so, not only did I sell hundreds of copies of Determined and Dangerous when it first launched, but it hit number one as an Amazon bestseller in 11 categories in just the first four hours.

I was completely blown away.

That was the first moment I began to be more open to change. And what happened next was even more eye opening. Those potential clients that I'd previously been talking to about coaching them to start their businesses and who had chosen to work with other coaches came back to me and said: "Chloe, I noticed you've just written your book, and it did really well. Can you show me how you did it?"

And that was the second big change and shift I had in my business. It was there and then that I realised that what I'd been doing for years as a business coach wasn't working and so, I asked myself: "Do I have the knowledge and expertise to publish a book? Well yes, I've just done it for my own book. Do I have the coaching skills to help someone else do it? Yes absolutely. Did I really enjoy the journey of writing my own book? And do I think I could do it again? 100%"

So, without hesitating, without allowing the limiting beliefs to come in, without panicking, without overthinking it, without letting my fear of change get in the way… I said yes.

Within three months, the number of clients I was coaching on starting their business had dropped, and the majority of our clients were now working with me to help them write and publish their own books. That was when Inspired By Publishing was born.

That was arguably one of the biggest changes I made in my business and to say that it paid off is an understatement. Now let's be honest, I didn't jump ship straight away and switch from business coaching to book writing coaching overnight. That was a bit risky for me. It took me about two years to let go of business coaching and jump into the book writing and publishing business.

As I'm writing this chapter, Inspired By Publishing has published 52 bestselling books and it's been an absolute whirlwind. And it all started when I finally gave myself permission to let go of what I thought I had to do and to be open to change. Because in reality, we all have opportunities for change.

I believe that we are all given opportunities every single day to make changes in our lives, whether that's starting a new business, pivoting in our current business, letting go of something that's not working or welcoming something new into our lives. The key is being open to change.

Making Change Easier

Change is everywhere, and we always have opportunities to change.

When I look back letting go of my old business and really leaping into becoming a book publisher, arguably the biggest change in my business, there were two very clear things that I had in place that helped me be open and ready for that change:

1. Certainty; and
2. Permission

Certainty

It's normal to be fearful of change because it's uncertain, it's the unknown and that can feel scary at times. So, it may sound obvious but the first step to being open to change is to find some level of certainty. This isn't necessarily waiting for everything to look perfect before you take the leap but to create your own certainty in any way you can so that the change doesn't feel quite scary.

Back in 2017 I struggled with severe anxiety and depression and one of the ways I managed the anxiety was using a simple technique which can help with creating your certainty.

Ask yourself:

- Realistically, what's the worst that can happen? Can I handle this, yes or no?
- Realistically, what's the best thing that can happen? Can I handle this, yes or no?

If you know you can handle the best and worst case scenario, that can help to create a sense of certainty within the change you're considering.

Notice the key word in the questions is "can I handle this?", not "will I be happy with this?" or "do I want this?" It is intentionally about whether you can handle it. It's about reminding yourself that you can survive it, no matter what happens. For example, if you want to start a business but are worried it might fail, the realistic worst case scenario is possibly the business not working out and you having to get a job. You may not be jumping from the rooftops about this outcome and it's obviously not the ideal outcome you'd have wanted, but could you handle it? That is the important question. When you realise you can handle *most* outcomes, it helps to create certainty in yourself to make that change.

Another way to get certainty is from seeing proof. If you can't find certainty in yourself, then process it and ask yourself, what needs to happen here for me to feel certain in this area?

Do I need practice?
Do I need to learn more?
Do I need to understand more?
Do I need to research more?
Do I need to experience more?

If I hadn't published Determined and Dangerous with success, giving me certainty through knowledge and experience, there is no way I would have been open to that change and help other entrepreneurs to write and publish their books too.

Permission

Once you feel like you have some level of certainty in the change, the next step is to give yourself permission for it to not work out the way you'd planned.

I know you're probably thinking that's a bit of a harsh way to look at change but giving yourself permission to fail isn't about predicting your failure, it's about being ready for whatever comes.

Many entrepreneurs feel like they have to get everything perfect the first time and that often sets us up for challenges, disappointment and procrastination. We can't control our results, we can only control our actions. So, when making a change in your life or business, you've got to give yourself permission to make mistakes. Give yourself permission to not be perfect. You don't need everything to be perfect for you to make a change.

If you wanted to write a book and you'd been waiting for the right time to get started, then give yourself permission to start without the perfect situation. Don't wait until you've got a week off in a beautiful hot country to write your book by the beachfront with no distractions, because realistically those opportunities don't come along very often.

And the longer we wait for the perfect situation to make a change, the longer we delay the results, for us and our clients.

Change doesn't have to be a quick thing. Take your time and give yourself permission to get it wrong. It's okay. You're human! Remember, change is inevitable. It's part of your journey.

Life is like a video game, you complete a series of challenges on the first level, you can't stay on that level forever. Often there is a final challenge you need to overcome to move onto the next level. It might be harder, it might be more challenging, but it is inevitable to be able to keep moving forward and growing into the person you know you can become.

So, if you're reading this chapter and thinking you need to make a change, maybe you're running your own business and you know you need to make a pivot, maybe you know you want to write a book but you haven't quite got there yet, or you're thinking, "Oh, I just don't want to change", well, let me leave you with this:

The longer you leave it, the harder it will get. The fear will kick in and the chances of you making that change get smaller and smaller as the tick times on.

Instead, trust yourself, trust your gut. Find the certainty within you and give your permission to go for it. If the change is meant to be, it will happen either way. Because change is inevitable.

You've got this!

About Me

I'm a number one bestselling author, international speaker, multi-award winning entrepreneur and founder of Inspired By Publishing.

After being in the coaching industry for years and struggling to make it work, I wrote and published my first book "Determined and Dangerous" in 28 days. After it became a number one bestseller in 11 categories, I was inspired to start my own book publishing agency and help entrepreneurs to write and publish their bestselling books.

The more I jumped into the publishing industry, I found myself being frustrated with the way the traditional book publishing industry works and I decided to shine a light on the industry and the dangers that entrepreneurs face when trying to get their books published.

Now I'm on a mission to help entrepreneurs to write and publish their bestselling books so that they can be seen as the authority that they are, stand out in their industry and get more incredible clients to work with.

Never Knew Me Until You

Sunna Coleman
Writing Coach & Author
Writers Inspired

"You will find yourself again. There were two people born that day."— Jessica Urlichs

Sleepless nights. Growth pains.
Miracle moments. Hope regained.
Unpredictability. Energy all drained.
Milestones hit. Proud accomplishment.
No time to rest. Time overstretched.
Tears of pure joy. Tears of utter frustration.
All the emotions. A complete evolution.

Some of you may read this and think instantly of the ups and downs of running a business. Others might pick up on the universal experiences of parenthood. Both are incredibly challenging journeys to go on that never leave you the same person as when you started.

When I first got into business, I had no idea what I was letting myself in for. I thought running a business would be all...

business. I didn't know that in order to be successful in the long run, you need a really strong foundation that actually doesn't start from the bottom line in your business; it starts even further back than that – from you, the founder.

For a business to thrive, it needs a strong, reliable, adaptable, skilled and grounded leader. But as humans, we aren't usually built like that as default. We come with baggage, wounds, scars, inexperience. It means that there's a lot of introspection to do as a business owner in order to start to build the strong foundation that will hold the business (and yourself) up through the inevitable knockbacks that will be encountered.

Whether it's lack of financial support, vicious competition, hard to reach clients, limiting beliefs, or something else, you need to be able to take each obstacle head-on and get back up when you're knocked down. After all, your business will only be as strong as you are.

Why do you think that the majority of the world's most successful entrepreneurs invest in their own personal development? You only have to listen to a handful of interviews with these leaders to notice the pattern. They each understand the resilience and level of vulnerability you need to be able to become a successful business owner.
So, where do you begin?

Untapped Unconscious

After my first few years in business as a writing coach, I thought I was getting a handle on things. That was until I broke down in tears in front of a room full of strangers.

I was at a business workshop, practising the art of personal and brand storytelling and delving into what drives me. I was rattling off my childhood stories of being highly creative, into painting, drawing, songs and story writing, when the coach stopped me and asked me, "But why?"

I looked at him blankly. "Why what?"

"Why were you so creative?"

"I just… was."

"There must be something that drove you towards creative outlets."

I wracked my brains as the rest of the group looked at me expectantly. I couldn't think of any elaborate reason at all.

Sensing my struggle, the coach tried to help. "Were you rebelling against your parents perhaps? Did they want you to be more academic?" he asked.

A little annoyed, I responded, "No, my parents were laid back about my interests. They let me follow whatever path I wanted."

"You need to dig deeper." Why? Why? Why? He kept probing.

And then it hit me like a ton of bricks.

It was like something in my mind and body had been physically unlocked. Suddenly it was clear as anything that the reason I was drawn to creative pursuits was because I was not safe to express my emotions or thoughts as a child. My father had anger issues and going against his beliefs and wants was dangerous territory.

So, I turned to writing, art and music because they were the only ways of letting my feelings out without obviously voicing my opinions. I needed to channel the energy somewhere. It was my real pain masked as something made up.

What led me to break down in tears? It wasn't that I had repressed my childhood experiences, I was very aware of them and spoke about them openly with people close to me. It was that I never had the realisation that it was all connected to what drives me as a person and to my purpose in life. It was a whole new level of understanding myself, and therefore, my business and the bigger impact I could have now that I was aware of my true driver.

After exploring this deeper understanding of myself, I was able to pivot my business and messaging in order to truly align with my bigger purpose. I went from just helping anyone write with more confidence, to specifically helping people find their voice and share their story so that they can positively impact thousands of lives. My brand and mission became a whole lot stronger.

If you are already in business, chances are you know the uncomfortable level of vulnerability you need to have in order to do personal development work such as this. It holds a mirror up to you and reveals every flaw.

It's a tough exercise to keep putting yourself through but if you can learn to persevere and keep an open mind, it shapes you into someone far happier, more confident and stronger. This makes you much more likely to be able to help others through your business.

You have to take care of yourself first before you can successfully lift anyone else up.

Taking Off The Mask

I know what I have shared so far is easier said than done. When I first started personal development training, I was very resistant to the idea. Not only was it uncomfortable to do but it went against everything I thought I knew about being an entrepreneur.

I thought I had to have a strong facade, be emotionless and neutral. Why would anyone buy from someone who shows weakness?

For example, I absolutely hated public speaking so I always made sure I was overprepared. I had pages and pages of notes as I didn't want anyone to get an inkling that I didn't feel like I knew what I was doing. I dreaded people being able to see through the front that I put on and realising that I was totally uncomfortable and nervous.

So when I needed to film videos or speak publicly, I made sure everything was expertly planned. I knew exactly what I was supposed to say and when. I just had to cross my fingers and hope that no one would stop me to ask a question and put me off.

When Queens In Business was launched, I mentioned an upcoming talk that I had to deliver to the co-founders. To my surprise, they gave me the complete opposite advice to what I had been doing. Don't plan. Don't write notes.

Everything in me was telling me that they were wrong. All five of them. But then again, I had seen them speak publicly and they all did such an amazing job. They didn't come across as nervous at all. Was the secret really to 'go with the flow'?

They put me on the spot to practise one of our upcoming talks in front of them. This was over a Zoom meeting so I was pleased to sneakily pull up some notes I had already prepared for this on the side of my screen. I rattled off my carefully planned points.

When I was done, pleased that I had pulled it off without them realising, Chloë said, "Great! Now try again without your notes."

"How did you know?" I asked.

"It was too perfect."

How can you be too perfect, I thought. But, in the safe space of just my co-founders watching, I thought I'd give 'going with the flow' a try. I was not convinced that it would work at all and thought, after they see how terrible I am without notes, they'll change their minds.

At first, I had no idea where to begin. I found myself trying to recall what I had written. I cursed myself for not having memorised it all. Stumbling through my talk, I finished and felt justified that I was correct in relying on notes and that they were indeed all wrong.

"That was better," Chloë said. "Now try again, and try not to think about your notes at all. Just speak."

Why wouldn't she let it go?! It's not going to work, I thought.

I tried again. This time, I just thought about the topic and spoke. I knew my main points anyway, I just needed to elaborate. After I was done, all the co-founders were smiling.

"Was that any good?" I asked tentatively. I had surprised myself. It hadn't actually been that bad and once I got going, putting my notes out of my mind, I spoke more naturally than ever.

"SO much better!" they replied. They could tell it was less rehearsed and therefore less robotic.

That small moment taught me a big valuable lesson. I realised that being human and letting down your guard creates a much more powerful connection between people. Being relatable and vulnerable is the greatest way to effectively reach more people and change more lives. No one can relate to perfection .

I was even more surprised to learn that it's okay – in fact, encouraged – to let an audience know if you are nervous, not feeling on top form, or if you're doing something for the first time.

When I first spoke on a live stage, I shared this vulnerability and found that instead of judging me, they instantly warmed to me. I was like most of them. Nervous in front of a big crowd. It made them want me to do well. If I stood up there claiming to be perfect, they would notice every imperfection like stumbling over my words. But since I honestly said that I was new to this, they didn't expect perfection and instead supported me.

The funniest thing is, once I had shared vulnerably, the pressure just lifted off me and I actually spoke comfortably knowing that I didn't have to be perfect!

Think about it. Who do you admire in business and what drew you to them? Is it an emotional connection to their story (their challenges, their downfalls) and/or what they stand for? I wouldn't be surprised if most of you said yes. Emotions are what move people to take action and connect deeply. It's a powerful persuasion tool.

Since then, I have ditched the notes. I only plan my key points and then talk around it. It allows for much more flexibility and a natural delivery.

If you had told me a few years ago that I would be speaking comfortably on stage I wouldn't have believed you one bit. I was never going to be a speaker. That just wasn't me.
How very wrong I was.

World Turned Upside Down

Several years into business, I was immensely proud of the personal development work I had done and what I had accomplished since doing so.

My business was my baby, requiring an incredible amount of my time, energy and investment. It had thrown everything at me and polished me into a shiny new version of myself. I had never been so confident in who I am, what I stand for and what my purpose in life is.

And then along came a real baby.

Any parents reading this will know that my identity, values and beliefs were all about to be turned on their head, shaken about into disarray and reexamined in minute detail.

During the pregnancy, I had it relatively easy. I felt mostly on top of things (apart from some baby brain) and the super planner in me had a return-to-business plan all laid out and ready. I intended on easing myself back in after the first three months (I wonder if any of you parents laughed reading that).

I know every parent's journey is different and you certainly can go back to work as early as just a few weeks in. But the reality is, you can never truly plan with a baby. You don't have any control over how the birth will end up going and how you will feel or how the baby will be coping post-birth.

You also can't prepare for how it will completely change your life. No matter how many people tell you about it or describe what being a parent is like, you can never understand the depth of it until it happens to you.

When you meet your baby for the first time, in an instant, everything is different.

The Jenga blocks of your life and priorities that you have spent so long carefully building tumble down in anticipation of being put back, never in the same order as they were before.

For me, the first four to five months were a complete write off when it came to thinking about work. All I wanted to do was ensure that I spent as much time with my daughter as possible. I couldn't even imagine anything else mattering.

My boundaries got even stricter and my time more precious. In business, it can be easy to let work seep into time that you thought you would be spending with family, friends, resting or doing something else you love. Having a baby was a great way to properly prioritise my time and shed anything that wasn't adding enough value to my life. Most of all, I became more selective and efficient with my work so that I could protect quality time with my family.

The biggest change applied to my working pace. I was well-known in business for being incredibly adept at juggling many ventures and never missing a deadline (it's the super planner in me!). But after having my daughter, I was forced to slow down. With a young baby requiring so much of my energy, I couldn't deplete it further by spreading myself too thin across multiple business opportunities.

At first, I felt a loss for the person who I once was. I felt like I wasn't as capable or successful as before. I tried to be both versions of myself at the same time and ended up feeling like a failure of a mum and a failure of a business owner, not being able to give either the correct amount of attention.

On the other hand, my daughter became such a strong driving force for me to do the things I had always wanted to do – like finish and publish my first novel. I wanted to be a great role model for her, showing her what she is capable of achieving.

It became clearer what I wanted to give my time to and what things I could take off my plate. Letting go of some things that once had seemed so important to me was very difficult to do but when I finally did, I had some room to breathe again. With a more focused approach, I could plan my time properly to achieve in all areas of my life.

Letting Go And Embracing Change

As someone who likes to feel in control of situations, having structures and plans in place, I have struggled with change.

But the big moments in my life from the adventures of business and motherhood to unprecedented times like the global pandemic have forced me to adapt and taught me the benefits of a flexible attitude and open mind.

I once feared change and held onto the past. But with each evolution of me I learned that I wasn't losing who I once was but gaining a new level of depth. It's like getting to know yourself better and what more you are capable of every time. If you stay stuck in the past, you don't evolve.

You won't get anywhere if you stick to what you know and stay in your comfort zone.

Change can be scary because it's uncertain. But what's once uncertain becomes your new comfort zone once you explore it.

Keep growing, keep challenging yourself. Without that, you stall. True fulfilment lies in adventure and discovery.

About Me

I am an award-winning writing coach and Chief Editor/co-author of the Queens In Business international best-selling book series. To date, I have coached over 50 entrepreneurs in book writing and have thousands of published works to my name, including bestselling mystery fiction novel, Her Empty Chair.

During my decade as a writer, I have interviewed the likes of Shaun of the Dead director Edgar Wright, actor and filmmaker Aziz Ansari, renowned chef Heston Blumenthal. I have created content for top brands such as Calvin Klein, Karen Millen, Ted Baker, Revlon, Lindt, Hotel Chocolat and many more.

But all this recognition came against the odds. Growing up, I was led to believe that I didn't have a voice. That what I had to say didn't matter. Writing was my escape. From short stories to songs, I used the power of words to transform my pain into creativity.

Through a lot of personal development and facing my demons, I have embraced the power of change to find my strength to speak up and share my writing with the world. My mission is to inspire you to stop living in fear – of your own limiting beliefs or of the judgement of others – so that you can escape your comfort zone and live the life of your wildest dreams.

I dedicate my chapter to my husband and daughter who support and inspire me to make positive changes every day.

Entrepreneurship Is An Inside Job

Shim Ravalia
Award Winning Entrepreneur
The Gut Intuition

"In any given moment we have two options: to step forward into growth or step back into safety." – Abraham Maslow

Change is the only thing that is always constant in your life because without it, there is no growth, there is no scaling up or upgrading.

Ever had a time in your life where the change you needed to make was so painful but you knew that staying the same way or in the same place would be even more painful?

You see, whether you are looking to start a business or develop another one, or maybe it's just an idea you're considering at the moment, entrepreneurship is an inside job.

What do I mean by that?

I mean looking at all the great and the ugly versions of yourself to truly understand, accept and become a better version of yourself that you are unconditionally proud of, no matter what. No amount of the typical business books or business coaches out there ever told me this fun fact and I am here to show you the way to facilitate change with humour, resilience and strength.

Let me take you back to more than 12 years ago where I distinctly remember waking up one morning feeling this wave of heaviness and unfulfillment coming over me. The thought of going into work felt flat as a pancake and it took a lot for me to just get up and go. I had spent a long time working in different health clubs and gyms since graduating from university and it was all very exciting to go out and use my degree to start earning some money.

But I couldn't quite shift that uncomfortable feeling of being comfortable. Feel familiar?

I had been feeling like this for a while and I thought that there had to be more to life than just getting paid every month for the set hours I've worked, saving money for a rainy day. I even had a savings account called 'The Rainy Day' as well as a pension plan too. There was just no stimulation and nothing exciting to look forward to other than get paid, paying my bills, requesting time off in the hope I could get the dates I wanted and doing the same thing month after month. I mean, a hamster wheel probably sounded more exciting to be on than that. But then, I realised I was on one.

Every day was groundhog day!

I remember very clearly a conversation I had with myself in December 2011 saying these very words over and over again, "Something has to change." 2012 arrived and I began my year visiting India with my Mum for a couple of weddings in the family. Towards the end of my trip I was in Mumbai for a couple of nights before heading back to London when the phone rang with my brother on the other end. This conversation was where my entrepreneurial journey really actually started; where the seed was planted.

He shared an opportunity with me that totally changed my lifestyle. He told me that the gym he used to go to was going under new management and there were a couple of offices available to rent. "You should totally start your own business here Shim, your own sports therapy clinic, think about it." A part of me was smiling ear to ear and another part of me was trying to work out how I was going to make that happen.

I didn't have a business degree, or any experience in creating and building a business from scratch, let alone an example to truly follow. It was an uncomfortable feeling of the unknown at first and I liked it, I liked it a lot.

On the plane home, I was literally day dreaming about having my own office, making a shit tonne of money, imagining a long line of clients, not having to work weekends anymore and having this sense of freedom of being my own boss and not having to listen to anyone's rules. Yeah… it felt good, felt good indeed.

Within 24 hours back from my trip, I was already viewing the office and checking the place out. It was perfect, I could visualise straight away how it was all going to work out and I just accepted to take the room and open my own clinic. My next step was to tell my boss that I no longer was going to work for him anymore. I honestly dreaded it because we got along well and I enjoyed working there because of the people rather than the job itself. However, boredom set in for me and there wasn't any room to grow or learn anything new within this position anymore and it was time for a change.

Within 30 days, I set up my first ever company on Companies House, handed in my notice to my boss , gathered my family around to help me come up with a name for my business and got one of my cousins to help me design my company logo.

Of course, the changes I was making were uncertain, I was anxious most of the time thinking to myself on whether it was going to work out or not. But it was the action taking that made me feel a lot better and more confident and just have my own back at all times. For the time being, this was enough to start with and I wasn't overly concerned that I hadn't sorted out a leaflet or had a website running.

During my last 30 days in my job, I spent many of my lunch breaks sitting in the coffee shop planning, creating, building, visualising on how to execute my plan.

What did I really believe in?

Why was running a business now so important to me?

What were the solutions I was going to offer?

Who am I going to help?

Where were these people I wanted to help?

What would I charge for my services too?

Oh it was such an exciting time, I felt so alive because of my creative juices being in full flow. I felt like I was putting my brain to good use whereas before the routine of a 9 to 5 job was just brain numbing to me every single day watching the clock and waiting for home time to arrive. Mind you, I did enjoy the copious amounts of coffee with my work colleagues just to pass the time.

I ran it successfully for six years. Now I want to tell you what the so called gurus don't or won't tell you, along with the lessons you can learn on what to do more of and avoid:

#1 Hustling Is Overrated

I hustled, meaning I worked many weeks and months seven days in a row. I was exhausted but the money looked really good in my business account and it was good cash flow. I paid myself well and bills were paid on time. However it was at the expense of my health; lack of sleep, food and water because I just crammed in as much as I could to make the money I needed. I learnt from an early age to never go in the red with money and to create safety with my finances no matter what. This worked in the 9 to 5 scenario but not when I ran my own business. I had to embrace and learn the many ups and downs that came with running a business. So avoid the work hard, play hard mentality because in the long run, it will cost you more in health tax and you won't be in a fit state to do anything let alone run a business.

#2 Don't Be A Martyr

I simply ran the first three years of my business by myself with no staff. My mindset at the time was just to save as much money as I could so that I could pay myself on time every month. Financial security has always been a big deal for me and still is. I wore all the hats you could have when running a business and looking back at my journey, I sometimes wonder how I really managed everything by myself. I was the marketing manager, the finance manager, looking after the social media channels, looking at budgets, overheads, content calendar, the admin, taking the business to the next level. I had multitasking mastered down to an art. I was so good at it. But at times, it was exhausting and if I didn't do it there would have been a backlog of admin to catch up on every day. Safe to say, I was a control freak with both hands in the business and I just didn't want anyone else near my business. It was all out of irrational fear anyway, the fear that they will take my clients and set up their own thing. It never happened yet the biggest lesson here is: So what if they did? You are unique and they are not you. My advice is get a really good coach or mentor who has got the results you want and invest and build a team slowly but surely and delegate the tasks you don't have the key strengths for.

#3 Your Business Is Limited By Your Health

The biggest and easiest change I made in my journey of being an entrepreneur is my health. My business was limited by my health! Fact! You can kiss your ideas or business projects goodbye if you don't move and upgrade your health practices consistently every so often.

If you have ideas or know that you want to upscale your business in some way, ask yourself whether your body can handle it? Is it fully equipped to handle the amount of stress that may come with the change? I burnt out so many times running my first business that I guess it felt 'normal' because everyone that I knew did and wore it like a badge of honour. It was almost worrying that if you weren't busy being busy, something was seriously wrong which is not true. Listen to your body and if you need to rest, then rest. The best thing I ever did was schedule my time off and rest days into my diary so that I knew it was coming.

So whatever you do; whether you have a busy week or not, slow down to speed up because your body and your brain will thank you for it in so many ways.

Sometimes, less is more.

#4 Your Intuition And Logic Are Your Business Navigators

I believe that the true essence of entrepreneurship is deeply rooted within yourself where intuition and logic act as essential navigators. These internal navigators will guide you as an entrepreneur through the unpredictable times of business, helping you make decisions that align with the business that you would love to create or are creating already.

Your intuition is your subconscious mind's ability to understand and react without conscious reasoning, playing a really important role in entrepreneurship. It is the silent force that will help you recognize opportunities that you might overlook. Your intuition is developed through experience and an acute awareness of the surrounding environment. During the pandemic, my intuition served me very well. With so many unknown changes ahead of me, I followed my gut feeling when on paper everything was uncertain so logically I would have gone more towards safety. Yet, your intuition is very deeply rooted inside of you and often can be a little whisper as well.

Your logic, on the other hand, is the systematic and analytical aspect of decision-making. It involves critical thinking, structured problem-solving, and evaluating necessary data. Your logic ensures that decisions are made based on rational thinking and evidence, which provides a healthy balance to the often unexplainable nature of intuition.

The synergy between intuition and logic is what I strongly feel makes entrepreneurship a holistic and dynamic pursuit therefore an inside job. They are complementary forces that drive entrepreneurial success.

Entrepreneurship is way more than just making money, market analysis, competition, and financial planning. It's the glorified, instagrammable shit that these so-called gurus portray these days that can often leave a part of you feeling that you don't have enough, taking action from a place of lack rather than good intentions.

You can listen to as many podcasts as you want, read as many books as you want and invest in as many business coaches as you want. However, nothing truly ever tells you the truth other than your intuition and your body. This is really key in business to look at things and yourself from the inside out.

Remember, entrepreneurship isn't a straight vertical road, there are many roads you may take to get to your destination so be adaptable to those changes that lie ahead for you in an environment where rapid changes can often occur.

Remain open to new possibilities and adjust which is vital during uncertain times.

Remember, the best business GPS isn't found in an app, but within your own gut instincts and sharp and focused mind. Trust your inner compass, and even when the road gets ugly and bumpy, you'll laugh through the detours and celebrate the unexpected victories, high-fiving yourself for dodging disaster after disaster; having this profound realisation that you've just invented a new type of speed bump.

After all, if entrepreneurship were easy, everyone would be doing it—and we'd all be billionaires by now, sipping margaritas on Necker Island with Sir Richard Branson, riding unicorns to work, paying our bills with monopoly money and the guarantee of free pizza every day!

You've got this ;)

About Me

I am the Founder of The Gut Intuition and I help business owners and entrepreneurs go from stress to unlimited energy and razor sharp focus without burning out in health and in business.

I've had the pleasure of being featured in many well known publications like Business Woman Today, CBS News, Fox, NBC and ABC to really spread my message and my vision about health for the future of entrepreneurs all over the world. Most recently, my company was recognised to be the best health and wellbeing facility in Greater London too.

Born and bred in East London, and coming away from university with two degrees in Sports Rehabilitation and from here I worked in gyms and leisure centres until I found my entrepreneurial path.

Having been an entrepreneur for over 12 years now, I have been through many ugly bumps along the way and had my sanity tested through testing times. Embracing the changes that are unexpected and unknown is what grew me to be the entrepreneur that I am today. I hope that this book instils you with a lot of faith and knowing to keep going when times do get difficult and know that it's just temporary, knowing you will come out of it a different, stronger version of you ready to take on whatever comes your way.

All In the Name Of Change!

Tanya Grant
Founder
The TNG Designs Group Limited

"Change is made of choices, and choices are made of character."
– Amanda Gorman

Calling all lost or confused entrepreneurs who once had a clear vision for how they were going to reach their goal but now have an unfocused, foggy sense of direction that makes no sense at all because the idea of change has messed up your plans and progress!!!

Hahaaa, if ever there was such a call out line for your marketing, it wouldn't surprise me just how many people could actually resonate with that. And whether you can relate to it with what you're currently experiencing or have now overcome, this chapter and what I'm about to get into, is still for you.

Why?

Because you're an entrepreneur, business owner and/or someone who is ready to make a difference in your world... Well before having been thrown for a loop that is. I'm here to help get you back on track and I'd like to start by way of this chapter.

At the time of my writing this, it'll be 22 years of my having worked in the design industry and it's fair to say that I've seen and experienced my fair share of change too. Some good and welcomed. Some not so good and quite frankly I could put two fingers up to!

Now as much as I'd begrudgingly admit that most change, if not all, is actually necessary for a sense of progress to be realised, I've equally come to realise that there's at least four different types of change that have the ability to impact our lives in the craziest of ways.

There's the type of change that....
1. you're looking for
2. forces your hand
3. is inevitable
4. is unexpected

And not only that, as much as we attempt to prepare ourselves for moments that involve those unexpected changes in particular, it's those that still have the ability to really slap us in the face when we least expect it.

I'll be deep diving into a few experiences of my own based around these types of changes shortly and I'll also be sharing with you tips that I wish I'd known before being confronted with my experiences of change. What I hope for you, is that with all of this in mind, it will help to prepare you as much as possible on your continued entrepreneurial journey, for any pending pop-up slap-in-the-face moments.
So here we go…

#1 The Type Of Change You're Looking For

This first type of change is typically welcomed, being that it's the one you're looking for. However, it can be a little cumbersome when it comes to the results you actually receive.

Now all of these changes reflect a sense of personal growth but this one in particular resonates more with it, as the change you're looking for searches for a more intentional outcome so that you can develop and progress in your world.

Key "trigger statements" to look out for when identifying this type of change involve words like I need to… I want to… I have to… I'm ready to…

More specifically put:
I need to sort out my life and get things organised.
I want to make a difference.
I have to do something.
I'm ready to make a move.

For me, the change I was looking for included that latter phrase and if you've read any of my previous chapters in the Queens In Business book series you'll know that I've often spoken about the phrase, "What needs to happen in order for you to make a move?" This was my trigger and essentially what made the idea of me being ready to make a move, start. Making what I do work better for me business wise, I mean.

Now, I've said before that it was at that point that I was actually ready to start hearing the answers that were flying at me, so much so that I now welcomed them and made the effort to just get on and take the action that was needed to move my business forwards. But what I didn't share with you was that my newfound intention for my reaching this 'goal of greatness' began working against me.

It was during the height of the pandemic where everyone was on lockdown. The world was turning upside down but I was on my mission to get shit done! I got so obsessed with it and worked, what I can now say was too hard. I didn't take breaks and sat at my laptop thinking that I was building a better foundation for my brand so I needed to 'keep going' when in actual fact I was worsening the state I was in.

Have you ever felt a pain anywhere on your body, so much so that you thought if you give it a few days it'll wear off with a painkiller or two? I had severe pain in my lower back and that's what I did. I took some painkillers and instead of the pain subsiding it got worse.

It was an obvious sign of burning myself out, and it worsened into a condition which caused me to sporadically spasm with any movement I made. It's not a pain I'd ever felt before but I know for sure that I wouldn't wish it on my worst enemy! The simplest of things took the longest of time for me to do. Walking felt like I was running a marathon and turning over in my bed seemed like it took forever. And it took for that to happen, all so that I could learn how to simply stop.

Hahaaa I actually had no choice, as for a few days even sitting down was a mission in itself. So I surrendered to it…

I put myself in time out, listened to my body and started taking one day at a time to recover slowly but surely. It took me about three weeks to get back into working order and in that time I had to reassess the change that I was looking for. So…

Instead of just wanting to make what I do work better for myself, my goal was to not only do that, but do that with the intention that I wasn't going to hurt myself in the process or disrespect my boundary for self-care. This is what I'd like you to consider too.

It comes with a warning though.

Know that the different future scenarios or changes you're looking for will test and cause you to push the border of your chosen boundary. Also, you might catch yourself repeating old habits and could even break your own protective rule so you may want to choose a few more boundaries to help back your main one too. How quickly you learn to be aware of what's about to happen will be the making of how quickly you can learn to stop, put yourself in a time out, listen to your body and take one day at a time.

Ask me how I know this :)

#2&3 The Type of Changes That Force Your Hand And Are Inevitable

Now I've deliberately clumped these two together because although they do carry their own separate characteristics, they equally go hand-in-hand too. You'll typically see these changes as a result of anything from career structural changes, technology advances or market trends to relationship dynamics, natural disasters, and sadly death.

Whilst there are no distinct, key trigger statements for them, there are the "trigger responses" you have after suddenly experiencing them, coupled with a few proceeding words, that will give the tell-tale signs of the type of changes you're in.

For example:

Response: ***shocked emotion***
Proceeding word/s: ***Wait, what?! / Oh no! What's going to happen next? / Oh shiiitttt, what am I going to do now?***

I'm going to pay specific attention to career structural changes, for this one.

I don't need to tell you how often these happen, and I wonder if in fact, this could have been the deciding factor for you wanting to start your own business and build your brand in the first place? Although it wasn't necessarily my deciding factor for starting my own business, it did play a role in my wanting to make things work better for myself using the knowledge I already had. Here's how it played out for me.

I've spoken about my story before in one of my earlier QIB chapters but there's a few things I want to elaborate on here. My career in the designing world started as my wanting to get my foot in the door as a graphic designer. So, in 2004 that's exactly what I did. I became a freelancer in my profession and secured roles in some of London's leading marketing houses.

This continued to the end of 2015 and like with most roles out there I experienced a lot of ups and downs during that time. Ups whereby the money and opportunities or projects worked on were great, and aside from encountering an odd character of two, the people and contacts I made along the way were great too. As for the downs, now those were interesting.

More so in the sense that because during that time, I saw so many (what I can now describe as) racial biases. I'll be talking more about that specifically later. Just know that it made for more than an uncomfortable feeling.

Another down point I experienced was my not feeling secure enough in making sure that good money kept coming in. I found it tiring constantly being on the lookout for my next position and didn't always have a contract lined up after finishing one that I was working on. It made me feel uneasy as well as uncertain so I sought out permanent work, because that's where I believed I could find the security I was looking for.

Fast forward to February of 2016 where I landed a permanent senior designer role. I felt like I finally got the security I was looking for. Although at first challenging, everything went off to a flying start where I was getting on with my team, the clients, suppliers and progressing nicely. There weren't any signs to tell me otherwise, so when I was called into a meeting with my creative director, exactly a year later, I was none the wiser about what was about to happen.

Let me start, by asking you, have you ever felt like you've had the rug pulled out from underneath you?

Well, that was how I felt when I was told that not only was my role going to be made redundant, but I was also going to be demoted to a lesser paying role too. I had three days to choose whether I wanted to stay in the company and just as I referenced those trigger response examples before, that was exactly what I felt and all of what I said when I found out the news.

I went backwards and forwards with what my decision was going to be, and I wonder if you've ever been in a position where the decision that you should have made was the opposite of what you chose to do? It was for me.

I decided to stay. Why? Because even though I knew what the consequences were, I wasn't done yet. I hadn't achieved enough of the client facing experience I wanted at that point. I said to myself, "Stay if only for a while, then leave after you've gotten what's needed. It won't be for long."

As time continued in this new dejecting role, I got the experience I was looking for all whilst still knowing in the back of my head that I needed to make what I do work better for myself as remaining in this space wasn't it. And this was where my hand became forced as the inevitable continued to happen in the background. You see, despite what I was going through, redundancies were happening companywide, and in some cases, others were being completely let go. So, what happened six months later didn't even come as a surprise. It was literally inevitable.

I was called into another meeting with my creative director only to find that this time my role had now been made fully redundant. Needless to say that this time, I was over it. In fact, it was the happiest I'd been in that role in a long time. Did I feel rejected, downhearted, unworthy or even inadequate? Nope, not at all. I was free.

Free to get on and do all the things I should be doing so that I can make what I do work for myself. And here's what I'd like you to take away from this. When you go through change, listen for and receive the answers that force your hand to make decisions you've been putting off for a while. Know that they're going to happen anyway and yes, you'll be fine when that time comes too.

#4 The Type Of Change That's Unexpected

This final type of change, the one that is unexpected, includes the common scenarios that involve pandemics, disruptions, natural disasters, downturns, accidents, job loss, bad health, and emergencies.

Just like changes 2 and 3, these also have trigger responses, however this time phrases reflect those that are shocked and starting with "what" , "why", "how" or "really" come into play.

For example:
What The F?!***
Why now???
How did this happen?!
Really?!

All self-explanatory I'm sure you'll agree but when it comes to this type of change, I'd actually like you to consider something completely different here.

I'd like you to think about the idea of direction and more specifically, the unexpected or even unplanned direction that can throw a spanner in the works and change your trajectory for how you move forwards with building the awareness of your brand and business.

Let me explain.

When I mentioned to you that I wanted to make what I do work better for myself in the previous change points, what I didn't realise was the magnitude of how far that statement could actually take me. I put that statement out in a prayer to God, for you it may be the universe or the equivalent of a higher power, and the direction that I ended up going in wasn't down the traditional mainstream graphic designing path, it was one that involved branding, a clear message that I wanted my audience to know about, and equally be empowered to go on and make purposeful changes on their own too.

And it's that latter part that I really want to get into here.

You see, often the average business owner and entrepreneur will lead with the 'operation' or 'tool' of what it is that they do. They will only tap into the surface level of what their service or product can offer but not necessarily the way it will make their audience feel after having experienced it. The 'tool' in my case was graphic design and where others have their equivalent and go wrong in my opinion, is where I believe they need to understand that there's more value needing to be added to get the eventual results they're looking for.

When I discovered that my unexpected change was transitioning into the likes of branding, I was able to pull together the reason why I was really doing what I do. This is where my helping others to see that they are more than what they see, stemmed from. And it's evolved since then too.

Now to say this additional turn and specific direction came as a shock would be an understatement. It opened my eyes to see even more and it's still one of my favourite past times that I loved welcoming because of what it really means. But it was something that had to be shown to me so that I could acknowledge the true power of what I really have to share with others.

Remember when I wrote about some of the downs I was experiencing in the previous points #2&3, namely by way of racial biases? Well, those experiences of being overlooked, silenced by, and not feeling like I had a valid voice, was what I can now say, became the underlying tone of influence for why I do what I do. There's so much in my story that others can relate to, and at first, I didn't really appreciate that. But then this happened.

I was delivering a keynote in person session on stage in May 2022, advocating all things branding to an audience of like-minded change makers, business owners and entrepreneurs. A woman came up to me after my talk and shared with me how seeing me in my expert position inspired her. She, we'll call her "J" for short, was also a black female leader in her own right. J saw me stand as an authority figure on stage, showing up as "me" rocking a then short stylishly shaped afro, being taken seriously and who more importantly, showed her the possibility of what she could do too.

J mentioned to me that not only did she resonate with my shares, it also made her realise that she needed to be doing more to get her own voice out there. She saw in me what she could be. I was her example. And this is what I now help others to understand for themselves too. You see, I look forward to the day when women who look like me can be seen as the norm in spaces where we were the minority in or wouldn't otherwise appear to "fit in".

That being said, these are the takeaways I'd like you to have for not only working with this type of change but also dealing with the unexpected layers it may have for you as you go through its process. Firstly, don't fight against an unexpected change. You'll wear yourself out trying to prove why it's not for you so just be open to receiving the value it brings and work with it. Lastly, with this change, let it encourage you to show up as the example that others need to see. You're not just about your service or product, there's more to it so help others to understand what that is too.

And that's it. Four types of changes, realisations, takeaways and solutions for how when you feel like you're getting thrown for a loop and have lost your focus for reaching your intended goal, you can take a step back, realise the signs, and prepare yourself for your continued journey ahead as you get yourself back on track.

Remember to watch out for those warnings. They've got a nasty habit of distracting you from moving forwards!

About Me

As a diversity and inclusion champion, award winning solution-based brand specialist, a multiple international number one best-selling co-author, speaker, Queens In Business Co-Founder and Founder of The TNG Designs Group Limited, I'm a huge advocate for branding and why representation matters.

I've written this chapter for those who have hit a confusing or disruptive bump in the road and are stuck as to what to do to help move past it. I was in your position once so know how much of a distracting shift it can cause.

I've spoken on stages and many podcast interviews on the importance of these topics and how building up your visibility and status can have a great impact on how people see you as an authority in your industry. I've worked with many SMEs as well as collaborated with global brands such as Topshop, Topman, Dorothy Perkins, and Miss Selfridge, so it's fair to say that I know what it takes for a brand to become noteworthy.

I started my career as a freelance graphic designer over 22 years ago at the time of my writing this, during which my past experiences have taken me through many adventures. I've witnessed a mixed bag of career driven highs and sadly demoralising lows that have included prejudices, and later, a redundancy in 2017. This became my trigger for wanting to make more of a name for myself as the go-to expert in my field, and to stop being the best kept secret. I've been able to turn what would typically feel like discouraging rejections into the movement of my greatest journey yet.

After having officially registered my business in 2019, I have since evolved into an inspiring brand specialist, motivating others to realise that they are more than what they see and why representation matters. Throughout my work, I instil my Group's primary values of Guide, Grounding and Growth. Through branding, I help service-based business owners in the coaching space to stand out from their competition, make better connections and build better authoritative reputations so that they can win new business and more.

A Life By Design

Chris Hill
Co-Founder
Lifestyle Entrepreneur

"When you change the way you look at things, the things you look at change." – Wayne Dyer

I am going to describe two people to you, and I want you to tell me the difference between them with the information I have provided.

Person one is overweight and although he understands the value of his health, he has never really given much consideration to his own. He is however known to be a loving and caring person, who will always go above and beyond for those around him to ensure they have everything they need to be happy. Having left school with a limited education, he has thrown himself into the working world and currently holds three jobs. His full-time job is a forklift driver, which he commits 40 hours per week to in a shift pattern, as well as working two part time jobs as a chef, and as front of house staff in two different pubs. He left home when he was sixteen years old and currently rents a room in a three bed house share.

Person two is fit, healthy and emotionally well balanced. He is a father of two, a husband, and a serial entrepreneur. He is also known for his desire to help others and bring laughter and happiness to their lives, and has a natural ability to connect and communicate with most people he meets. Professionally, he works hours that suit his lifestyle so that he is able to maintain a healthy work-life balance, which allows him to raise his children alongside his wife. He has designed the life he lives today and is confident that he will continue to create abundance of his own, and the lives around him.

Now you know a little about these people, I would like you to answer these questions before you read any further on:

How old are both people?
How does each person view themselves?
Which would you rather be?

Before we move any further, let me introduce myself to you. My name is Chris Hill and I am the Co Founder of Lifestyle Entrepreneur, a business dedicated to teaching people how to build businesses that support their lifestyle, rather than take over it! I have been an entrepreneur for the last 15 years and have built and scaled multiple six and seven figure businesses, as well as holding high level positions in the corporate space such as Global Brand Manager. You might not believe this, but we have actually met before, and it might surprise you as to where.

It was at the start of this chapter, because both person one and person two are me, just from very different stages in my life. Version one of me was back when I was in my late teens to early twenties, whereas version two of me is the thirty-six year old who is writing this chapter today. So what happened in the 15 years between person one and person two to allow such a change in circumstance? And how does that help you in your onward journey to your own successes?

In this chapter I am hoping to answer those exact questions, and share with you the key changes I made in my life to take me from where I was to where I am today, in the hope that you can apply it to your life to replicate my success in building a life by design. Whether you are at the start of your journey and looking for the change that will kick things off, or whether you are further along and want to continue your development, this will be relevant to you.

When I wrote the description for both person one and two, I recognised both of them as if independently they were both a reflection staring back at me from the mirror. These people could not be more different but as I crafted their bios it was like talking to two individual people as if they were both here today. The reason for that is because in reality, they are. Both of these people are versions of me that still exist in some capacity today, and it is because they share so many similarities.

Both versions are uneducated (in a traditional sense of qualifications), both versions share the same deeply rooted desire to help people and improve their lives and they also both possess 90% of the same skill sets. I honestly believe the two versions are very similar, and to the people who have known both I think they would agree with me also. So how has version two come so far if fundamentally, it is the same person in the driving seat and how can I help you have the same changes in your life in just one chapter of a book?

Naturally, there will be multiple changes that will have happened as I have traversed the 15 years, but what I want to share with you here is the ONE fundamental change that has been the contributing factor in step changing my life, so you can replicate that success in your own. The change I am referring to here isn't something physical, it isn't educational, it is actually something a lot simpler, and that's perspective.

The biggest change I have made is the perspective I take on both myself, and the environment around me, and with that simple change it has allowed me to break down the walls and ceilings that once held me, and replaced them with momentum and success.

Perspective is such a powerful tool for change, and for the rest of this chapter I am going to teach you the three main perspective shifts and strategies that have been used to accelerate my journey and have ultimately changed the game.

Strategy One - Halt! Imposter!

Imposter syndrome is a term bandied around in personal development A LOT, and if you have ever experienced it yourself it can be crippling and debilitating. If this is the first time you have heard this phrase this is how it is defined:

Impostor Syndrome or Phenomenon: A psychological experience of intellectual and professional infraudulence.[1] It is "the subjective experience of perceived self-doubt in one's abilities and accomplishments compared with others, despite evidence to suggest the contrary.

As those who want to develop and improve, regardless of whether that's as people, employees, leaders or entrepreneurs, we naturally reach as far and as high as we can. The Human race is pre-programmed to want more in life, to accomplish the next milestone or scale the next peak, (it is the reason we are at the top of the food chain) so why is it when you summit and find ourselves in new surroundings, do we feel like we do not belong?

We forget all of the hard work and effort that has gone into the climb, the lessons we have learnt and the challenging ridges we have navigated, and at times, we are left feeling like at any moment someone will point a finger to shout "HALT! IMPOSTER!"

I believe it is because, although we scale the mountain, when we arrive at the top and are surrounded by others who have achieved the same feats (and sometimes more), the reflection looks back at us in the mirror, the climber who is still at the bottom of the mountain. Your internal voice is screaming at you. "I must have fluked the climb, I shouldn't have made it this far" and you are left with that feeling of being found out.

The reality is, you have scaled the mountain, you are in the right place, but your perspective is yet to catch you up. Your perspective is still of the person who was at the bottom of the climb, who had things to learn before they could complete the climb. That perspective then leads you to question whether the person you were did all the work needed to finish the climb after all. Surely you haven't and there are some skeletons in the closet to discover? This is the beginning of the downward spiral.

If it continues, the likelihood is your self belief will drop and things that once seemed easy will begin to become challenging. You will become critical of little mistakes you make which only positively reinforce the fact that you are indeed an imposter. The other reality could be that you start this process earlier on, and instead of progressing and trying the climb you believe that you have more work to do on mastering your current position before you are even worthy of attempting to summit. Do either of these sound familiar?

Hero To Zero

At some stage, imposter syndrome will show up in all of our lives, some of us will have the natural ability to deflect it by 'winging it' or 'faking it until we make it' while for others it will become a real problem. So how can we avoid it all together so that the journey to success continues for as long as we desire in the right direction? For this, I can share a three-step strategy that has always helped me realign my perspective. It's called Hero To Zero.

Step One - Acknowledge Your Surroundings

When imposter syndrome strikes, you are usually going to find yourself in surroundings that seem alien to you, but you have some level of skill to survive in. The thing you used to do once made you the hero, but now you have started at the bottom of a new challenge. It is time to acknowledge that your surroundings are different and you are no longer at the top of your game. Shift your perspective from master to student and begin to learn everything you can about the terrain and the gaps in your knowledge. If you can, find a mentor who can guide you in the early days who has the knowledge you are lacking to help you fill in the gaps.

Step Two - Vulnerable, Not Victim

If you feel like an imposter, it is tempting to defend your previous hero status from previously executing at a high level. DO NOT become the victim, instead open yourself up to being vulnerable and asking for help and feedback as you learn and adapt. As elements to the new environment appear, if you have never encountered them before, lean into the fear of asking questions and trust that none of them will be 'stupid'. The quickest way to adapt is to educate yourself.

Step Three - Shift Your Perspective And Your Audience

It is important that you leave the old version of you behind, and that you shift your perspective to where you are TODAY. There is a reason you are standing where you are and there will be a ton of others who have watched your climb and agree that you nailed the journey. If you are struggling to believe it for yourself then find the people who can believe it for you and ask them what it was they saw that made them feel that way. The more cheerleaders you have, the louder they chant, and it's hard to hear the negatives of imposter syndrome over a rocking party in your name!

Question The Comments

There is a second, deeper strategy that for some will seem more challenging, but when I say this is the key to unlocking a step change in your perspective I am somewhat understating it. This strategy started my journey to success, and it took me YEARS to realise I even needed it. Even then, it took the outside perspective of my wife to bring it into my mind's eye.

As humans we have five key senses that work in harmony, that were essentially designed to keep us alive (sight, smell, touch, taste and hearing). Yet today the majority of the population find we are no longer at risk of predators, and so these senses have been turned more to pleasure than protection. Which is why, in my opinion, I believe we no longer use them to their full potential. Hearing especially is one of the senses that isn't just underused, it can actually land us in quite a bit of trouble, especially when we hear so much without questioning what it truly means.

I'm not talking about the sounds we hear, for those who are able bodied and can hear well, the world of sounds that surround us can be heard crystal clear like a symphony to the soul. The thing that I am questioning is do we actually LISTEN? This strategy is going to get you to revisit moments that have shaped your perspective, so that you can understand if what was said is what you actually heard. This strategy is called: Question the Comments.

Step One - What Did You Hear?

There will be moments in your journey where you have shaped a perspective about yourself based on comments others have made. In order to change your perspective, you first need to acknowledge what has built it in the first place. There will be lots of contributing factors but a large piece of the puzzle will be what others have contributed via conversations or comments that you have held onto. The first step is to find the ones that have contributed most to your beliefs or perspective.

Step Two - Do You Remember?

In order to understand what was meant by the person, you are going to need to engage them in a conversation about when and what was said. This comment or conversation might have happened hours, days, weeks or years ago, so it is important to remind the person in order to ensure you are both speaking about the same thing. You can do this by saying: "Do you remember when we were [Insert place] and we were discussing [insert topic], you said to me [insert what you heard them say]."

Step Three - What Did You Mean?

In this step you are going to ask the person what they meant, but you are also going to tell them what you understood by it. Depending on the comment and the person, this might be an easy or difficult conversation, and I am happy to tell you the more tricky the conversation, the more likely it will lead to a fundamental change in your perspective. That is because the more we care about the person we are speaking to and the effect their words had on us, the more scared we will be for them to validate that we heard them correctly. Most of the time, however, the thing we took away that has shaped our perspective so negatively was never what was intended to be heard, and by discussing it, it will open up a whole new perspective for you to grow with.

Even in the rare instances when the comment was intended as it was heard, there is room to grow and shift our perspective by asking for more feedback on the subject and where the person sees how we could work with or around the subject to improve.

The Fundamentally Flawed Path To Failure

For years, when I wanted to be successful I was told to vision my success to make it a reality or to put positive affirmations into the world and the universe will deliver the results. There was a part of me that liked this idea, which was the creation of intentions that you wanted to meet, and I believe having a clear vision of what you want is key to reaching your goals.

I didn't believe, however, that if I were to put a picture of a Porsche on my vision board, a mystical creature of the universe would pull up to my drive and deliver one. There are, however, whole books written on the subject of affirmations and setting intentions which is why it is such a popular subject and ritual with so many uses.

The issue I have with it is that I have witnessed many people, who positively affirm the life they desire and the person they want to be, and the universe is not delivering it, which is where I had my perception change on the strategy.

When you set an intention or goal, it is a target, a line in the sand to aim for or the destination of your success. This is a physical point in which upon reaching, you will realise the fruits of your labour and be able to celebrate your success. With affirmations, on the other hand (which go hand in hand), it is speaking aloud to the universe from the perspective of that successful person that has already achieved those things. This is an example of an affirmation: "I am a healthy, wealthy person who has found love in life and has the ability to create abundance in all I do."

Now look at this thought through a different lens, the lens of the brain rather than the heart and soul. The heart and soul knows and absorbs the desires, and leaves us with a powerful energy of the person we might become. The brain, on the other hand, takes a more logical approach, realising these things are not a reality, and begins to serve up reminders of how far away we are from them.

Affirmations for the heart are viewed by the brain as being built on a lie, they do not exist and so logically the brain will serve up reasons that they do not. This inadvertently leads us to question if we are good enough to achieve our goals and in the worst case scenario even our fundamental skill set, which leads us straight back to... imposter syndrome, which creates a glass ceiling in our own minds.

If you want to create monumental change in your world, the best thing to do is to start with the destination. Work out a clear plan and roadmap to achieving it, and as you travel that journey, constantly realign and change your perspective of your now.

The reality is, today, you are the most perfect version of you that you can be, and nothing will change that. That is because you are the only version of you that exists, you are unique in this world and the only person who truly knows what you are capable of is YOU.

If you can walk away from this chapter and set your destination, plan your route and change your perspective to be able to cross the starting line, the change in your life will follow.

About Me

I'm a thirty-six year old father, husband and serial entrepreneur who values lifestyle and family above anything else. Many entrepreneurs are seen as gifted or born with talent, whereas my journey took a different route to the top. I left school with limited education and zero direction on where to take my life, but by following my moral compass and adapting to the world around me I was able to change my perspective and create vast wealth and happiness in my life.

I decided to contribute to this book to speak to all of the readers who are, or have been, in a similar position. If you long for more in life but are stuck with the belief that you could never achieve it, I am here to help you see that ANYONE can be successful. Regardless of background, education or any other factors. There is a path to success for us all, you just need to change your perspective. If this is you, my company Lifestyle Entrepreneur is a place you can be among like minded people who are looking to build a life by design, on their terms.

Rewiring Your Brain

Taiba Bajar
Award-Winning Researcher &
Licensed Brain Health Trainer
Autism Brain Empowerment

"You don't become what you want, you become what you believe."
– Oprah Winfrey

"You need to look for a Special Educational Needs school for your child."

"Your son needs noise cancelling headphones, that will help manage his symptoms."

"You shouldn't expect too much from your son, he will obviously struggle his whole life."

These are some of the unhelpful comments I heard about my son when he started showing severe autism symptoms after his skills regression at twenty months old.

I was worried. His skills regression meant that he lost words, lost eye contact and began to show severe anxiety to familiar situations. About 40% of parents with children on the autism spectrum report that their child experienced a regression in skills between the ages of eighteen and thirty-six months, after initially developing normally.

Like any worried parent, I contacted my son's GP and Health Visitor who added him onto the waiting list for physiotherapy, occupational therapy and speech and language therapy. I was lucky, I only waited two months on an NHS waiting list before my son's first physiotherapy appointment that lasted for 30 minutes. After an assessment, the physio said she needed to see my son every eight weeks for a 30-minute appointment.

Is that it? I didn't think that would be enough to make a real difference to him. A 30-minute appointment every eight weeks definitely would not be enough time for my severely anxious child to warm up to his therapist.

I was constantly worried, shared all of my worries to anyone who would listen, and I was met with pessimism. I felt like every health professional and preschool teacher that I spoke to wanted me to accept that my child would have lifelong struggles, and that the most loving thing that I could do was to accept this. They advised me to begin making accommodations for my child like purchasing noise cancelling headphones or looking for a specialist SEN school.

It's like they had given up on changing my son's fate and wanted me to give up and lower my expectations for him too.

But I'm his mother, I can't give up on him. This is not the dream that I had for my child and I wasn't going to change my dreams for him so easily.

Before having children, I studied dentistry at the University of Bristol where I also studied neuroscience and neuroanatomy. I remember learning how only 75% of a child's brain is developed by the age of three and 90% is developed by the age of five. My son was three years old so I knew that I had a chance to change this, why wasn't any health care professional communicating this to me? Surely, if I capitalise on this growth window and create an environment where he can learn as many skills as possible, it will rewire the connections in his brain, form new ones, and reduce the expression of his autism symptoms.

I want to make it clear that there is nothing wrong with having autism symptoms. However, seeing my son struggle with being in public spaces, unable to regulate his hunger or sleep, and lacking the skills to play with other children made me sad. This wasn't the life I wanted for him.

That's when I remembered learning about neuroplasticity from dental school, which means that a person can rewire their brain because all brains are plastic. This means that if the inputs to a person's brain change, their behaviour can also change. Clinging to this knowledge, I knew that I had to take action to help my child myself. I felt like I was the only one who could, and the only one in my son's life who cared enough to try everything.

I was always an avid researcher. I knew my way around scientific literature and was the only student in my year group to win the Alumni Clinical Research Prize at university for my independent research into student learning styles. I put my research hat back on and learned everything I could about the biological causes of autism. I learned so much about gut health, everyday toxins in our environment, methylation, cerebellum growth exercises and more. Why wasn't this information more readily available?

I worked with my son everyday. I deliberately changed his environment, worked tirelessly to expand his diet and to take him into environments which I felt would benefit his brain health. To the average person, if I explained how much I worked with my son, they would have assumed that I am raising my son to become an Olympic athlete, but they didn't know my son's daily struggles with meeting his everyday milestones. I would have been happy if my son was just meeting his developmental milestones, eating a balanced diet and no longer wetting himself everyday.

After 12 months of limited to nil progress, something clicked and my son began talking in sentences and he became conversational. He was making friends, he learned how to jump and run, and his meltdowns started happening less and less. This experience aligns with what I know about neuroplasticity. At first, creating new neural connections in the brain requires tremendous effort as you build a new pathway. Over time, this leads to a tipping point where the new pathway becomes the dominant way your child thinks, effectively rewriting their old patterns of thinking and behaviour.

The change I see in my son and all of the intentional effort I put into this transformation is my life's greatest achievement. Parents around me who saw this change began to ask me for advice about how to help their autistic child, and unintentionally I became the go-to person in my community for advice on how to help an autistic child.

I developed a 7-Step Autism Action Plan which I shared with parents but I had no intention on creating a business or going any further with this. I was employed and I imagined my whole life staying employed. Truth be told, I was comfortable in my employment and I thought I liked the predictability of employment. I had always admired entrepreneurs who followed their passions and bet on themselves to create a business, but I didn't have enough guts to do this, and I limited myself to accepting that I never would.

I was bullied quite consistently and quite badly as a child and this left me with low self esteem. It manifested in me with codependency relationships and with a binge eating disorder. I was always a slim child, but since childhood, whenever I felt low or stressed, I turned to the biscuit tin or the treat cupboard and finished whole packets of biscuits and chocolates in one sitting. I remember having this habit as early as six years old and it has stayed with me this whole time.

As I got older, I was juggling more stress and my metabolism began to slow down too. Getting older meant that now, whenever I felt low, I was able to drive to the nearest convenience store and buy whole family sized chocolate bars and finish them all in five minutes. I used to try and hide the wrappers from my husband, this habit filled me with shame. Only my closest friends and family knew this about me, as I only ever binge ate in secret. After having two pregnancies and a lifelong binge eating disorder, I was quite overweight and I accepted that I would always be overweight.

Discovering The Kindness Method

I'm one of the people who listen to The Diary of a CEO podcast, which is one of the fastest growing podcasts in the country. In one of the episodes , Steven Bartlett interviewed Shahroo Izadi, a behaviour change management expert, and she explained how she rewired her own brain to overcome a lifelong binge eating disorder. As I was listening to Shahroo talk, I felt like I was listening to my own life's story. I was awestruck and I related to her so much. After the experience with my son, I was familiar with neuroplasticity and rewiring the brain to change behaviours, but I didn't love myself enough to do this for myself.

I can't count how many times I listened to that Diary of a CEO episode on repeat and then one day I reached my own tipping point. I had two children crying upstairs, they were both overtired and I was alone at home and I needed to put them to bed. Normally in this situation I would open the biscuit tin and binge eat biscuits to help me cope with the immediate stress. Instead, I followed Shahroo's advice and grabbed a pen and paper and wrote down the self-talk in my head. I was shocked with what I wrote down.

I wrote words such as, "You're useless. You can't do anything. You're a waste of space. Just go away, you're such a loser and you can't do anything right." After I wrote these words down I was shocked at what I wrote. Until I wrote down my thoughts as I was heading to the biscuit tin for a binge, I was among the 90% of people who are not fully aware of their own self-talk and inner thought processes. 95% of a person's thoughts are on repeat. I asked myself whose words were these? They weren't my own words.

In my thirty-three years, I have never spoken like that to anyone. I then realised who these words belonged to. They belonged to my childhood bully as they taunted me and made me feel small and insignificant my whole life, and no amount of academic or professional achievement had changed that. I thought about the person who bullied me as a child. I still knew them as an adult and they were overweight themselves and quite lonely. As an adult, I would never take life advice from this person regarding my personal relationships or how to have a healthy lifestyle. Yet, I was completely unaware that their words were repeating in my head during my most vulnerable moments.

The more we live in a past memory and the more intense the emotions that are associated with that memory, the stronger those brain connections become. The more we repeat a thought or a behaviour, the more likely it is that those thoughts and memories will float to the front of our minds as a dreaded thought or memory even if we are unaware of it happening. The intensity of my childhood bullying experiences explains why the self-loathing and the binge eating repetition was a consistent habit for me.

Realising what I was saying to myself and whose words they belonged to changed everything for me. I was able to disconnect myself from my self-talk and changed how I spoke to myself going forward. Now whenever I felt low or stressed, instead I consciously changed my self-talk to speak to myself how I would speak to my best friend if they were ever low or depressed. For the first few weeks this was an intentional practice until that pathway in my brain changed permanently and this was now my new self-talk.

I shocked everyone as I refused late night eating and takeaways and I began to treat myself like I loved and cared about myself. What is more shocking is that after nine months of this behaviour change, I had lost four stone and I returned to the same jean size I wore at seventeen years old. An achievement that I never thought would be possible for me. Most of the women I knew were content just to return to their pre-baby weight after two pregnancies, let alone reach the jean size they wore in their teens.

What is most surprising is that this whole behaviour change felt effortless to me. Once I changed the self-talk in my brain, I didn't crave the same foods as I did before and I reacted differently to stress. I also lost all this weight without changing my exercise habits at all (something I don't recommend), but it was all through loving myself enough to change the food that I put in my own mouth.

Achieving something that I never thought would ever be possible for me changed how I viewed myself. I am blessed to have lifelong friendships, an amazing family and to feel part of a caring supportive community but I was always very uncontent with my career. Despite completing five years of dental school, I never worked as a dentist because I learned that I had dyspraxia while I was in my final year of dental school and my low self esteem meant that I allowed myself to get bullied out of the course by faculty and again I limited myself.

Having a Pakistani background meant that I was encouraged to retrain into a respectable profession such as accounting now that I discontinued my dentistry career choice. So I started working for a big four accounting firm and I completed my ACA qualification. I was bored pretty much the whole time I worked in accounting. I had never been more unengaged while at work, but I liked the people I worked with.

I then had an unhappy year at work. My department was sold to a private equity firm and the culture of the company had changed completely which meant lots of those people now left the firm. I wasn't brave enough to be one of them. This experience of being sold without my consent, as an employee to a private equity firm made me realise that employment may not be as predictable as I had thought.

The Launch Of Autism Brain Empowerment

A bad experience at work made me just question why I was still at this firm when everything I liked about it had changed. I was only thirty-three years old and still had at least another thirty-two years of my working life left. I naively let myself dream about a life where I am passionate and engaged in my career, and where I can become someone who I admire. Whenever I met someone who ran their own business I looked at them in awe; this was something that I always admired about people but I accepted that I wasn't brave enough or multi-skilled enough to do it myself.

However, was that still true for me? I had recently lost four stone, in a way that felt quite effortless, and achieved something that I never thought would be possible for me. Could I realise my own business dream? I leaned on a friend who encouraged me to go for it, and that was the encouragement that I needed. I followed her advice and completed a limiting belief exercise where I wrote down every single limiting belief that I had for myself in my personal life and my professional life, and then again I questioned what was the origin of that limiting belief, and was it even true or could I disprove it?

The last part of the exercise was to write down an affirmation which I needed to recite daily disproving the limiting belief that I had originally wrote. I ended up writing a list of over 40 limiting beliefs for myself and therefore needed to recite over 40 affirmations everyday as part of her recommendations. This aligns with what I knew about neuroplasticity where a pathway can not be deleted, it needs to be overwritten with a new one.

I created a vision board for myself that featured my own company, Autism Brain Empowerment. In this vision, I formally coached other parents of autistic children through my 7-Step Autism Action Plan. The goal was to empower parents to help rewire their child's brain, meet developmental milestones, and reduce disruptive autism symptoms. After launching this business I began to receive a lot of interest, and my program was being used to formally help lots of autistic children make progress towards their developmental milestones and my clients were happy to provide me with testimonials too.

I shared my story with a new friend who encouraged me to write a book. I told her, "Okay, maybe I will do this one day, maybe next year or the year after, but I can't do this right now." Another limiting belief. After establishing a regular program of journaling and addressing my limiting beliefs to the point where I recognised this thought as a limiting belief. The adaptive regenerative power and agility of the brain are incredible. When we feel trapped by our thoughts or long-established behavioural patterns, it's helpful to remember this. Even our most basic intrinsic traits can be rewired with intention and self-awareness. This allows us to create significant changes in our behaviour pathways well into adulthood.

So I began to alter the way I thought. I never thought of myself as a published author. That was someone else, not me. But I also never thought of myself as a YouTuber or as an entrepreneur, or as someone who would ever be able to stop binge eating. If I could do that, then I could do something else that I thought was impossible too.

I committed to writing 1000 words every day before I met with a publisher and shared my first draft of "Unlock Autism". The book was met with such a great reception and it became a #1 bestseller. In under a year, I had lost four stone, started my own business, had happy paying clients and written the first draft of my book.

The more I did new things, the more I rewired the connections in my brain, overwriting my old thoughts and behaviours with new pathways. I always knew about neuroplasticity, and I went to great lengths to apply this knowledge for my son when he began showing autism symptoms. However, it was only when I started practising self-love that I began using these principles to change my own behaviours and became more of the person I always wanted to be.

Neuroplasticity is available to everyone. Whether you are an autistic child with severe symptoms of self harm and aggression, or a burned out working parent in their mid thirties. Anyone can unlock the power of their brain's plasticity to change their behaviour.

We all suffer from repetitive negative thought patterns and behaviours that we are unaware of. We all have habits that we think make our lives easier, but they aren't helpful to our long term health or happiness. Becoming more self-aware and developing self-love can help you prevent deep emotions from limiting your life choices. This allows you to move beyond these obstacles and create a life you and your family can be proud of.

I want you to be able to wake up your brain and unlock its full potential so that you can make your life what you really want. It's time to turn off autopilot and make decisions necessary to move forwards.

About Me

I am the #1 bestselling author of "Unlock Autism." I am also an award-winning researcher and a licensed brain health trainer. I studied dentistry for five years at the University of Bristol, where I focused on neuroscience and neuroplasticity as part of my degree. I graduated with two science degrees, one in dentistry and the other in bioethics, from the University of Bristol.

After receiving a diagnosis of dyspraxia and autism in my final year, I changed my career path and worked in the corporate sector for over ten years. When my son started showing autism symptoms and experienced skill regression at 20 months old, and finding minimal help from the NHS and his preschool, I began my own research into the biological causes of autism. This research led to the creation of my 7-Step Autism Action Plan, which helped my son meet his developmental milestones and overcome developmental delays.

Following the success with my son, I founded a parent coaching business called Autism Brain Empowerment. I teach other parents my 7-Step Autism Action Plan in both 1:1 and group settings. Drawing from my professional expertise and personal experiences, I equip parents to guide their children in reducing autism symptoms, unlocking their potential, and fostering their leadership in the world.

"What Do I Desire?"

Mart Tweedy
Owner/Director
Canny Crystals

"What makes you itch? What sort of a situation would you like? Because, if you say that getting the money is the most important thing, you will spend your life completely wasting your time. You'll be doing things you don't like doing in order to go on living, that is, to go on doing things you don't like doing, which is stupid! And so, therefore, it's so important to consider this question: What do I desire?" – Alan Watts

Picture yourself standing at the edge of a cliff, overlooking a massive, endless ocean. The horizon is a giant, colourful canvas filled with endless possibility. Each wave that playfully laps against the shore carries secrets of dreams not yet spoken, wishes not yet made, and potential just waiting to burst into life.

This ocean is like the Universe, brimming with the magical energies that shape our world, just waiting for you to give them some direction with your clear intentions.

Now, think of your desires as little ships, all ready to set sail. But for these ships to reach their dreamy destinations, they need specific coordinates. This is where our adventure of manifestation kicks off – with the magic of being specific.

Just like a captain needs a map to sail the seas, you need to define your dreams with pinpoint accuracy to guide the Universe in making them come true.

Consider this chapter your trusty compass. Together, we're going to dive into the deepest parts of your heart, discovering what you truly desire. By learning about the power of being specific, you'll be able to tap into the Universe's energy, turning those fuzzy wishes into sparkling realities.

One of the most common messages I get on a daily basis is from people asking how they know what to manifest in life and that really is all down to you, because it's pointless me saying the more common things that people want in life, such as "money" or "love" if those areas of your life pose no issues for you.

We need to learn how to get specific and ask for what we want!

"What do I desire?"

This question sounds quite simple on its surface, but it invites us into the depths of our being, urging us to get specific, to uncover, and to articulate the dreams we wish to manifest in our lives. But not only that, it allows us to discover the paths that lead us to the clarity and specificity needed to bring our deepest desires to life.

The Power Of Specificity In Manifestation

The Law of Attraction teaches us that to manifest our desires, we must not only ask the Universe for what we want, but be crystal clear about it. The Universe responds to specificity just like a GPS system needing exact coordinates to reach a destination.

Why is specificity so crucial, you ask? Specificity acts as a beacon, guiding the energy of our intentions through the vast possibilities of the cosmos to materialise our exact desires.

When you're specific, you activate a powerful frequency to the Universe. It's like tuning into a radio station; the clearer the frequency, the better you receive.

Back in the 90s, we had to turn a dial and tune into a radio frequency, and if you didn’t get it just right, you would hear the music over the top of lots of crackling white noise. And just like this analogy, the more specific you are, the clearer your intention will be.

Now, you might be wondering, "Why is being specific so important? Can’t I just wish for happiness or success and call it a day?"

Pinpointing your desires is like adding rocket fuel to your manifestation journey!

The Cosmic Order: How Specificity Shapes Reality

Imagine walking into a bustling restaurant without looking at the menu. When the waiter arrives, you vaguely say, "I want something tasty." The possibilities are endless, and while you might end up with a delicious meal, there's also a chance you'll get something that doesn't quite hit the spot.

Now, think about how different the experience is when you know *exactly* what you want – a nice, juicy cheeseburger with crispy chips and a crisp, cold beer!

The moment you place your order, the kitchen gets to work, preparing your meal to your exact specifications. Manifestation works in much the same way. The Universe is like that restaurant, and your desires are the orders you place.

When you're vague, the Universe has a harder time delivering exactly what you want. But when you're specific, you set clear intentions that act as precise instructions for the cosmic kitchen.

This not only helps you get what you want but also speeds up the process.

The Science Behind Specificity

Let's sprinkle a bit of science into our magical mix. Neuroscientists have discovered that our brains are like powerful supercomputers; always on the lookout for ways to turn our thoughts into reality. This is known as the Reticular Activating System (RAS).

The RAS acts as a filter, prioritising information that aligns with our goals and desires.

When you're specific about your goals, you're essentially programming your RAS to focus on the things that will help you achieve them. For instance, if your goal is to buy a new car, suddenly you start noticing car ads, dealership promotions, and even opportunities to earn extra money. This isn't just a coincidence; it's your brain filtering out the noise and honing in on what's important to you.

Being specific sharpens this filter, making it even more effective. It's like giving your brain that detailed map to follow rather than a vague idea of where you want to go. The clearer the map, the faster you'll reach your destination.

But how do we uncover these desires that lie beneath layers of societal expectations, fear, and doubt? I've got a 3-step process that I use when doing this.

Step 1 – Self-Reflection

Begin with introspection. Journaling can be such a powerful tool here. Ask yourself two simple questions:

"What brings me joy?" and "What have I longed for but never pursued?"

Allow your imagination to roam without boundaries. Grab a pen and notepad or journal, and just answer these two questions.

Step 2 – Visualisation

Take some time each day to visualise your goals as if they've already been achieved. Close your eyes and imagine every detail – the sights, sounds, and feelings associated with your success. The more vivid and specific your visualisation, the more real it becomes to your mind and the faster you'll start seeing results in your reality.

At some point today, close your eyes and visualise your ideal day; you may choose this to be in five years, or even a decade from now.

What are you doing?
Who are you with?
Where are you?

Visualisation not only helps in getting specific but also ignites that emotional connection to your desires.

Step 3 - The 'Why'

For every desire, ask yourself, "Why do I want this?"

You *could* say that you want a million pounds in your bank account, or a brand new house to move your family into, but they're just wishes… Understanding the underlying reasons as to *why* you want something adds depth and commitment to your desires.

For example, it's not just the *house*, but the feeling of *security* and *family* that it represents.

It's not just the *money*, but what you'll be able to *do* with it and how much *time freedom* you'll have because of not having to work.

GET SPECIFIC!

This step is *so* important because it really allows you to tap into that raw emotion and express those feelings of what it physically means to you.

Crafting Your Manifestation Blueprint

With clarity on what you desire, it's time to create your manifestation blueprint.

Detail Your Desires

Write down your desires in as much detail as possible.

If it's a job, what is the position? The environment? The salary? The impact? Your colleagues?

If it's a house, where is it? How are your neighbours? What impact does it have on your well-being?

If it's money, what does it mean to you? What can you buy? How will it affect your mood?

Create Those Vision Boards

One of the most fun and effective ways to get specific with your manifestation is through vision boards. This method not only helps clarify your desires but also keeps them at the forefront of your mind.

When I mention this to people, the first image it usually conjures up is a huge, in-depth cork board with hundreds of cut-out images from magazines, pinned onto it – it doesn't have to be this taxing! Vision boards can be as simple as finding just *one* image that represents what you want and setting it as your phone wallpaper.

Start by creating a vision board – a collage of images, words, and symbols that represent your goals and dreams. This isn't an arts and crafts project; it's a powerful manifestation tool. By selecting images and words that resonate with your desires, you're sending a clear signal to the universe and your subconscious mind about what you want to achieve.

This is going to be such a powerful shift for you because you're going to be seeing that image 200-300 times a day subconsciously when looking at your device. Visual aids can be incredibly powerful. A vision board with images and words that represent your desires can serve as a daily reminder and motivator for *why* you want those goals.

Affirmations

Words are incredibly powerful when it comes to manifestation. They can shape our thoughts, influence our emotions, and ultimately determine our actions. This is why affirmations and declarations are such important tools in your manifestation toolkit.

Affirmations are positive statements that reflect your desired reality.

The key to making affirmations work is specificity. Instead of saying, "I want to be successful," try something more specific like, "I am thriving in my career as a graphic designer, earning £50,000 a year."

This detailed affirmation not only sets a clear goal but also helps you visualise what success looks like for you.

Declarations are similar to affirmations but are often more powerful because they're stated with conviction. For example, you might declare, "I am a confident and skilled graphic designer, attracting high-paying clients effortlessly."

The act of declaring your goals with confidence can boost your belief in your ability to achieve them, which in turn accelerates the manifestation process.

Craft affirmations that resonate with your specific desires. Repeat them daily. Affirmations reinforce your desires to the Universe and to your subconscious mind.

Manifestation isn't just about asking; it's about aligning your energy with your desires. So take heed of your mindset. Cultivate a positive mindset. Believe in the possibility of your desires coming to fruition.

Emotional Alignment

Emotions fuel manifestation. Feel the joy, the gratitude, and the excitement of having your desires fulfilled, even before they materialise.

Action

Take inspired action towards your desires. The Universe loves cooperation. Your actions signal your commitment and readiness to receive.

Navigating Challenges

The path to manifestation will be met with challenges. Doubts, fears, and impatience may arise, but that's fine, we'll get over them.

Overcoming doubts and fears is all about recognising these as part of the journey. Use them as indicators of what may need healing or further clarity.

Patience and trust

Manifestation takes time. Cultivate patience and trust in the Universe's timing. Remember, everything arrives at the perfect moment.

Breaking Down Your Goals

To get specific about your goals, you need to break them down into smaller, manageable steps. This process not only makes your goals more attainable but also helps you stay focused and motivated along the way.

Let's say your ultimate goal is to run a marathon. Whilst this is a great goal, it can feel overwhelming if you don't break it down. Start by setting specific milestones such as, "I will run three miles without stopping by the end of this month."

Once you achieve this milestone, set another, like, "I will run six miles without stopping in two months."

Breaking down your goals into smaller, specific steps makes the process less daunting and helps you track your progress. Each small victory boosts your confidence and reinforces your belief that you can achieve your ultimate goal.

Aligning With Your Desires

Specificity isn't just about clarity; it's also about alignment. When you get specific about your desires, you align your energy with what you want to manifest. This alignment creates a powerful magnetic force that attracts your desires into your life.

Being specific tunes your energy to the exact frequency of your desires, making it easier for them to come into your reality.

Overcoming the Fear

Many people struggle with getting specific about their desires because they fear disappointment. They worry that if they set a specific goal and don't achieve it, they'll feel like a failure. But here's the thing – specificity doesn't limit you; it empowers you!

By getting specific, you're not closing yourself off to other possibilities. Instead, you're giving the universe clear instructions about what you want while remaining open to the idea that something even better might come along. Trust that the Universe knows the best way to bring your desires to you, and don't be afraid to refine and adjust your goals as you go.

Practical Exercises

Now that we've explored the why and how of specificity, here are three practical exercises to help you get specific with your own goals.

Exercise 1: The Clarity List

Grab a notebook or journal and write down your top five goals. For each goal, answer the following questions:

What exactly do I want to achieve?
Why is this goal important to me?
How will I feel when I achieve this goal?
What specific steps can I take to achieve this goal?
What resources or support do I need to reach this goal?

This exercise will help you clarify your goals and create a detailed plan for achieving them.

Exercise 2: The Visualisation Journey

Find a quiet place where you won't be disturbed. Close your eyes and take a few deep breaths. Visualise yourself achieving one of your specific goals. Imagine every detail – where you are, who you're with, what you're doing, and how you're feeling.

Spend at least 10 minutes in this visualisation, fully immersing yourself in the experience.

Repeat this exercise daily, reinforcing your specific goals and strengthening your belief in their attainment.

Exercise 3: The Affirmation Blueprint

Create a set of specific affirmations for each of your goals. Make sure each affirmation is positive, present tense, and detailed. For example, if your goal is to improve your health, your affirmation might be, "I am healthy and fit, exercising regularly and enjoying nutritious meals."

Write your affirmations on sticky notes and place them where you'll see them often – on your bathroom mirror, fridge, or computer monitor.

Repeat your affirmations several times a day, feeling the truth of each statement as you say it.

Embracing the Power

Congratulations! You've just unlocked one of the most powerful secrets of manifestation – specificity. By being clear and detailed about your desires, you're not only speeding up the manifestation process but also aligning your energy with your goals.

Remember, the Universe is like a magical restaurant, ready to serve up your dreams exactly as you order them. So don't be afraid to get specific, set clear intentions, and trust that your desires are on their way to becoming your reality.

Keep using the exercises and tools discussed in this chapter, and watch as your goals transform from wishes into tangible successes.

The power of specificity is now in your hands – use it wisely and joyfully as you continue your manifestation journey, and just remember to ask yourself that question at some point today…

"What do I desire?"

Happy manifesting!

About Me

I'm a thirty-seven year old working dad of a four month old (and an eleven year old Jack Russell). Back in 2019 I suffered the biggest low point of my entire life when my Granda (Geordie for Grandad) passed away suddenly. At the time I was working in the mental health sector of the NHS and the irony was that I couldn't see a way out of my grief and depression.

In a brief flash of insanity, I called out for help to whoever was listening as I lay there in the bath one evening, and my spiritual journey began. I discovered crystal healing, mindfulness, gratitude and visualisation techniques, which all helped in digging me out of the bottomless pit I assumed I was in.

Just two years later, I decided to put all that I'd learned into online teachings, and with my last £250 in the bank, I launched my very own website cannycrystals.co.uk – which I thought may offer a little bit of extra pocket money each month.

By confronting my fears head on, and believing in my true worth, I was able to unlock something within me which I didn't think existed – the sheer will to make something of myself!

In just one year of launching my business, I was turning over more in one month than I had earned in the entire year for the NHS, and I subsequently handed in my notice to go fully self-employed. In the last three years I've turned over just shy of £750,000 and have managed to fully retire my Mam (who now works for me). My podcast is #1 in the UK for Spirituality week after week, and I now have over 30,000 people enrolled into my online academy based around spiritual well-being and self-development.

I now help people struggling with their mental well-being and ultimately empower them to find true meaning in their lives.

The Joy Of Collecting Experience

Annette Corbett
Clarity & Leadership Coach
Annette Corbett Coaching

"There is no greater agony than bearing an untold story inside you." – Maya Angelou

Once upon a time…

When I was a little girl, I wanted to grow up to be a princess. You wouldn't think so, now. I'm no girly girl, and you'll rarely catch me wearing pink. It must have been around the time Princess Diana was in the headlines every five minutes, so perhaps it's not entirely surprising. Although I was always more into fairytales than any factual reality. And anyway, that soon changed once I discovered jeans, ditched frills, and became a bit of a tomboy.

It took me quite a few years more to become a fully-fledged feminist who never wanted her identity to be defined in relationship to a man – prince or otherwise – but that's a story for another time. For now, let's get back to the princess stuff…

I would come home from school and change into a long dress that looked like some kind of Arthurian cosplay. I would spend my evening swishing around in it, making random things from paper, pens and glue. My mum must have had quite the job wrestling the dress away from me, so it could go in the wash.

Evidently, imagination and a love of storytelling have always been part of my life. To this day, I believe everybody has a story to tell. And too many stories go unheard, especially from women. As a coach, I see myself as helping women to tell their stories and to tell them their own way.

So, let's start by telling some of my own, and sharing some of the changes that have brought me to where I am.

What Do You Want To Be When You Grow Up?

I used to be jealous of people who could answer that question. Once you're past the princess/firefighter/astronaut phase, it gets asked a lot. And it's one that resurfaces at various points in life – sometimes with more urgency than others. Our education system funnels us into narrow channels from early on, as we decide on GCSEs, then A-Levels, then degrees, vocational training and then jobs.

There's immense pressure at a young age to choose a fork in the road. One that will likely determine the direction of the rest of your life.

If you know at fourteen that you want to be an accountant, an artist, or an architect, that's all well and good. Your options are clear. But, for me, there was never that clarity of vision. I knew what I enjoyed, even what I was good at but I had no idea what I wanted out of life. How to decide which door to open, when that choice means so many other doors would inevitably slam closed?

Perhaps that's why I ended up bouncing around different jobs and career paths like a pinball inside a machine for so many years. The existential fomo of committing to one particular path when I wanted to experience everything was just too great.

How I Developed My Superpowers

I want to pause for a moment to tell you another story. One about a little girl who knew how to hide. A little girl who learned that staying small meant staying safe. That academic achievement might equal acceptance and that being too visible might be dangerous.

That girl was me, of course.

The daughter of a primary school headteacher and jazz musician turned publican, I grew up surrounded by music, stories, and imagination. But the house I grew up in was also volatile, unpredictable, and frightening. The story of humanity is one of survival through adaptation. For me, that meant learning to spot any sign of change in mood.

As a child, I was an emotional barometer. Able to detect the slightest change in air pressure that might indicate an impending switch from affability to storming anger. The roll of an eye. The weight of a footstep. The too-hard slam of a door.

That's not to say that I ever felt lacking in love. On the contrary. In my coaching practice I talk about working with awesome women, and my mother will always be the template for the awesome love and support a woman can give to others, even in the hardest circumstances.

But I know that the changeable atmosphere of my childhood home had a fundamental impact on who, and how, I chose to be. I was a shy, quiet girl, introverted, even. I hid so much of myself in the interests of staying small. Of staying safe. But what I also know is that those early experiences gave me a valuable gift. My ability to anticipate, appreciate and respond to the emotions of others is part of what makes me such an effective coach.

I often joke about sharing a similar origin story to Spiderman. How hypervigilance became my Spidey Sense of empathy. I found my superpower, but I had to be bitten by a radioactive trauma spider to acquire it.

The World That Tells Us How To Be

Every story that we hear adds an ingredient to the recipe of who we are. It all goes to play a part in how we navigate the world.

As women, we've been told the story that only a narrow window of behaviour is acceptable. We have freedoms that previous generations of women could only have dreamt of, and yet so many of our beliefs are still framed through the lens of patriarchy.

We're weaned on a cocktail of misogyny, capitalism and systemic racism that closes doors to us before we even realise we might want to walk through them. We're taught not to be too much of anything, and yet that we can never really be enough. We learn that staying small means staying safe. That achievement equals acceptance. That being too visible might be dangerous…

The desire to be of service to others and the societal pressure to be supporters and nurturers are two sides of the same coin. In my coaching practice, I see how these twin drives towards selflessness were manifesting in shared characteristics. I refer to them as the three Ps: Perfectionism, People Pleasing, and Plate Spinning. In other words, doing all the things, for all the people, all the time and always to a high standard, of course. Everything, everywhere, all at once, if you like!

These are behaviours that informed so many of my own decisions. And I was seeing this triplet of characteristics replicated again and again in the women around me. It later became the focus of my coaching practice. But I'm skipping ahead again. Back to the story…

Still Playing Small, Still Playing Safe

I believe my own tendencies towards the three Ps contributed to my meandering route through life. I drifted from one office job to another, always conscientious, but never entirely engaged. Then, in 1996, my cousin – one of my closest friends – passed away from complications related to Duchenne's Muscular Dystrophy. It was one of those stark reminders of mortality, when such a bright light went out of my life before he had even reached twenty years old.

So, about three weeks before the start of term, I made the decision to study. I managed to just scrape onto an English degree. As someone who had always listed English as my favourite subject, it felt like an easy choice. It was an utterly delicious period of my life, learning to interpret the world around me in a totally different way. But, let's be honest, an English degree is… well, it isn't much of anything. A 'default' option that takes you nowhere in particular. So, that change from secretary to student reverted to secretary not long after graduation.

I think I always knew the nine to five of office life wasn't going to be enough for me, but I suspect I could have easily drifted through life as a Legal PA, earning decent money for relatively little responsibility. As it turned out, the universe had other plans…

The Call To Adventure

I'm not religious. I would probably describe myself as agnostic, at most. But there seems to be an outside force that has a way of nudging our lives in a particular direction. If we ignore those nudges for too long, it eventually resorts to giving us a good, hard push instead. For me, one of those nudges took the form of a nasty accident.

I was on a cycling holiday in France, travelling down a steep hill at high speed. I was caught off balance by the wake of a lorry passing too close. My front wheel wobbled, turned perpendicular. The bike stopped dead. I didn't…

The universe pushed me so hard it sent me over my handlebars. I was left with a broken wrist, badly sprained ankle, and scrapes down my left side that still show signs of scarring to this day. Gee, thanks universe. You have my attention!

In *The Hero With A Thousand Faces,* Joseph Campbell talks about reaching a point where we realise we have outgrown our lives. When our familiar beliefs and ways of being no longer fit and it's time to step over the threshold of our known world into something new. He refers to this as the call to adventure. That cycling accident was one of mine.

In that enforced pause from work, I was granted space to think. To reflect on how I was spending my time. What I wanted from life. In those six weeks, I decided that being a PA amending documents and managing diaries for senior partner man-babies was most definitely not it.

So, what did I want? I still didn't really know. Fortunately, I didn't have to wait too long before I had an idea.

What Happens Now?

It's surprising, really, that a girl who grew up loving fancy dress and the theatre never considered a career in the performing arts. While my wrist was still in a cast, I went to see a production called *The Masque of the Red Death*. A richly-detailed, building-wide immersive adventure inspired by the gothic horror of Edgar Allen Poe, by a theatre company called Punchdrunk. My mind was blown.

I went on to volunteer as a steward on the show, spending at least two nights a week in that dark and twisted fairytale inside Battersea Arts Centre until the show ended. That prompted a cascade of change, including a postgraduate degree in Arts Administration, quitting my PA job, and a series of roles in different arts organisations. Years later, things came full circle, and I ended up as a fundraiser back at Battersea Arts Centre. That's when the universe nudged me towards my next chapter.

BAC employed an in-house coach called Joanne Irvine to support the staff. I remember one particular conversation. I wasn't enjoying my fundraising role by then, but didn't know what I wanted next. So, I told her about my career path to that point, and everything I was interested in. She described my professional meanderings as "collecting experience."

A lightbulb went off in my head. She was right. But I also felt a weight of shame at what felt like wasted time. I was caught in a loop of growing and developing, but not **doing**. A library of learning, but to no particular end.

She suggested that perhaps having a sense of what I was travelling towards might help me understand what opportunities to take, and what to let go. That, if I knew my path, the detours would hold less interest. I knew that if I didn't make some decisions, my life would continue to meander absent-mindedly. I would keep feeling dissatisfied and unfulfilled. But which door to choose?

Where Were You When The World Stopped?

A global pandemic might not seem like the best time to start a business. Especially if your industry has almost entirely ground to a halt. But that's how my next chapter began.

When I changed career, the difference between the corporate and cultural sectors had felt immediate and stark. I'd moved from a world where hard work was well compensated. Paid overtime, staff discounts, subsidised restaurants. I'd even worked in a law firm with an in-house gym.

In the arts, I was seeing people working equally hard. Often much harder, in fact. It's an industry where people go above and beyond to make the magic happen. Where everyone carries their passion way beyond the confines of their desk, and that pernicious phrase, "the show must go on" translates into a culture of long hours, low pay, and blurred work/life boundaries.

The arts replicate the hierarchies of the corporate world, but without the resources, support and predictability that allows you to switch off at 5pm. And organisations are often led by similarly strong personalities, but unmitigated by robust policies and procedures, and with bad behaviour excused as 'artistic temperament.' I was watching a slow motion epidemic of burnout, overwhelm and exhaustion that was driving people towards mental and physical ill health, well before the onset of covid forced every venue in the world to go dark.

After my own experiences of workplace bullying left me feeling burned out and depleted, I became acutely aware of how women in particular were suffering in this exploitative culture where it was so easy for those driven by a sense of service to lose themselves.

In February 2020, I was having some inspiring conversations about developing a project to support wellbeing for people working in the arts. Then, within a month, everything imploded. Like so many others when the country went into lockdown, I became unemployed. All I could think about was how to make ends meet. But then, an opportunity came my way that finally addressed the question, "What do you want to be when you grow up?"

Finding My Flow

I remember the moment vividly. I'd qualified as a coach in 2019, and was a facilitator on a programme called Culture Reset. It was an amazing programme pulled together in the midst of lockdown, helping people in the arts to 'reimagine the future of culture' in a post-covid world.

I was supporting a cohort of eight cultural leaders across different genders, races, ages and geographies. At this point in the Zoom coaching session, they were sharing feedback on an exercise. Then something strange happened.

I had a moment almost of dissociation. A split second of transcendence where I stepped back and watched what was happening on screen. The conversations, insights, and ideas. The joyful openness and compassion being shown as people held space for one another. I experienced a wave of... something I can barely articulate. It was as if someone was calling my name.

I felt what I can only imagine an artist must feel like when they stand back from a painting and the entirety of the picture becomes clear. This moment, this act of creation that had been channelled through me, that I helped bring into being. It felt utterly magical. That moment changed everything.

That was when I decided to begin building a business around coaching and facilitation. The focus on women in leadership came later, but the seed was planted deep that day. Every skill, every experience, every story, even the residues of childhood pain and hypervigilance that had left me with such a keen sense of empathy. It all came into play.

From that moment, I knew **exactly** what I wanted to be. A coach.

Owning Up To Being Awesome

I've had the privilege of working alongside some amazing women in my life. Especially as a coach, helping women leaders in the performing arts, film and academia. I've seen how those women are often the engine driving truly transformational projects where everyone involved feels safe, supported, and seen – even when things get tough. It became so obvious how these talented and passionate women were fading into the background, while others with louder voices and more flashy job titles stepped up to take a bow.

These were the women I wanted to see in charge. Because these women – the ones who became my clients – were awesome. They tended to be the most creative, collaborative, and competent people in the room. But they hid their awesomeness in a cloak of compassion, always facilitating the visions of others to the detriment of their own.

Burdened by people pleasing and perfectionism, they were channelling all their energy into supporting and developing those around them, getting overwhelmed, and leaving themselves depleted, disillusioned, and drained. But stepping into their full awesome selves and looking afresh at their own needs and desires felt strange and frightening. They'd been listening to the external noise of expectation for so long, they could no longer hear themselves. And, when they did, it tended to be the voice of doubt and self-judgement that spoke the loudest. Because they'd learned that staying small meant staying safe. That achievement equals acceptance. That being too visible might be dangerous...

So their talents and visions got lost in *shoulds*, as they avoided the frightening uncertainty of trying something new and different. As they avoided *being themselves*.

Who You Are Is Always Evolving

Change is not a one and done thing. We don't disappear into a cocoon and emerge as a fully formed butterfly. It takes time. For some, life is a process of experimentation and exploration. A tentative trip down one path, a doubling back, a change of direction. That has certainly been the story of my life and my business.

I often think of it as like a jigsaw puzzle. Gradually building a picture of how I want things to be. Fitting it together, piece by piece. Then, every so often, something comes along to flip over the table, and scrunch up everything I've assembled. And I'm left sitting on the floor in front of a big pile of random pieces.

These moments are rarely fun. In fact, they usually suck. But, in my experience, these are some of the most important moments in life. For a while, things stay messy, uncomfortable, scattered. We lose sight of the picture altogether, in among all the chaos. But these moments of confusion are also an opportunity. Change often hurts, before it helps.

When everything is laid out on the floor, we can more clearly see the component parts that make up our life as it is currently lived. We can make choices about which pieces to keep, and to discard. If we give ourselves permission to be ruthless with our desires, these Marie Kondo moments of joy-finding are an opportunity to reassemble just the best of us.

This is often when women seek me out for support. When they're all but ready to scrunch up the jigsaw of their life out of sheer weariness and frustration. When they are being handed so many pieces, they no longer know which ones match the picture on the box.

I learned the painful way that the hard-earned self-reliance that is so often a symptom of trauma and people-pleasing can only take you so far. We can't – and shouldn't – go through these unsettling processes of change alone. Not when there's such power and comfort in having someone sit alongside us on the floor, rooting through that messed up jigsaw. Helping us find and assemble those corner pieces, those edges, those clear portions of sky, until we can make sense of the picture again.

Becoming The Queen Of Quitting

Like a fable, the morals we learn from the changes in our lives often only makes sense in hindsight.

Those small choices that impact on the immediate, but that may not gain significance until we re-examine them further down the line. Those massive decisions that feel like burning down parts of ourselves, and that send our lives forking off in an entirely different direction.

I think back to that idea of 'collecting experience,' and the emotions that insight provoked. That sense of shame at the different paths I'd wandered down, then abandoned, only to begin again. Now, I see all that experience as a source of power. Every moment has enabled me to better understand, and better help, the women who come to me, holding all the pieces of their broken jigsaw, and looking for support.

A while ago, I had a conversation with a former colleague about the work I do. How I help women walk away from situations that no longer serve them. I mentioned how this was not necessarily my client's explicit intention when they came to me, but how it often seemed as if, on some level, they had already made a choice. In coming to me, they were just wanting someone else to give them the permission that only they could grant to themselves.

He described me as the Queen of Quitting.

My first reaction was that the phrase could be a fantastic hashtag. But then I resisted, pushed it aside and returned to my usual way of working. After all, what HR manager would ever hire someone who describes themselves like that!?

But that phrase stayed with me. A seed was planted, and began to take root.

Even as I write this chapter, I feel myself on the verge of another nudge from the universe, as that seed begins to sprout. Here I am again, looking at that pile of jigsaw pieces, figuring out a brand new picture. I feel an invitation to step into something bold and expansive. Something that is both exciting and terrifying, like the best stories always are. And I can tell you now that, by the time you read this, things will be different for me. So, everything I'm sharing is simply what feels true to me now.

Get Comfortable With Discomfort

If I were to share one lesson from the convoluted route to building my coaching business, it would be this. I want to tell you that it's okay to collect experience. To change direction. That the pile of jigsaw pieces may take time to coalesce into a picture that makes sense again. Because **you will change**, like it or not. Whether you choose to resist it or to embrace it is what will determine the quality of your experience.

Your power lies in learning to get comfortable with the discomfort and uncertainty. In anchoring into that still, central core of you that knows who you are and what you want to bring to the world.

Despite all the changes, there is often a shining thread that runs through the narrative of our lives. Like my desire to help others tell their own stories. If you can find that thread, these changes of situation just become a shift in methodology towards that same end.

I am the sum of every single moment of my life, and so are you. Each experience and experiment, whatever the outcome, has made me who I am.

No matter how many times you start afresh, you are never starting from square one. You bring with you everything you have learned about the world, and about yourself. Each ingredient adds to the richness of the recipe.

Change is an iterative process. It is neither predictable, nor linear. The things that prompt our transformations are a web, not a straight line. A tangle of filaments that interconnect and influence each other in ways we can never fully understand. Each decision feeding into the next in an ever-growing network progress.

So, allow yourself the grace and space to change. Sit quietly in the in-between-ness of it. Listen to all that you have learned, and all that you have been, until you hear the story of what comes next. In that listening, you may hear a story that longs to be told. If so, please don't deny the world the brilliance of your full and glorious awesomeness.

After all, why settle for being a Princess, when you can be a Queen?

About Me

There are lots of ways I could describe who I am: a fourty-seven year old, perimenopausal, single woman living on the south coast of England. Lover of horror movies and science fiction. Daughter. Sister.

Then there's who I've been: goody two shoes, introvert, perfectionist, people pleaser. Well, I'm still some of those. Let's say I'm in recovery.

Professionally, I describe myself as a coach and cultural professional with over 15 years' experience supporting the arts, heritage, film and academia.

I founded my business in 2020 in response to the seismic shifts in the performing arts landscape as the pandemic took hold. It began as a creative consultancy, helping people gather in the spirit of collaborative curiosity. It gradually transitioned into something different.

In fact, transitions are my thing.

I've quit many things in my life: a corporate career, a long-term relationship, most recently my own hometown. I've gone from holding tight to what I know, to becoming quite the expert at walking away from what no longer serves me.

I've come to believe in the power of taking courageous leaps into the unknown. That's why I focus on helping women envision what that might look like for them. Those leaps feel so much more possible with someone holding your hand.

I help women dial down the noise of external expectation that has drowned out their inner wisdom, so they can give themselves permission to become the truly awesome woman they were always meant to be.

I want to acknowledge all those awesome women who have inspired me. Particularly my clients, who have helped shape my business into what it is today, and what I hope it will become. Change cannot happen in isolation. It occurs in the spaces between yourself, and those around you. You have been instrumental in changing me.

Transforming Trauma Into Triumph

Dan Todd
Trainer, Speaker & Author
Impactful Marketing

"I can't change the direction of the wind, but I can adjust my sails to always reach my destination." – Jimmy Dean

I'm nearly thirteen years old in the back of my dad's car on the way to the hospital for my weekly check up. I was listening to my first ever CD using my cutting-edge portable CD player with enough battery for about two hours (I feel old now)!

And the song playing is Mobile by Avril Lavigne.

The lyrics go…

Everything's changin' when I turn around.

All out of my control, I'm a mobile.

Those lyrics sum up life perfectly. It's constantly changing and it's mostly out of our control. The only thing we can control is how we handle it. It comes down to us. To a choice only we can make. And one that I had subconsciously made a few months prior to first hearing that song.

The Choice

When we're facing traumatic, negative and devastating change we're unknowingly at a crossroads.

Road one: Accept the change. Accept the trauma. Acknowledge it's bad. It's unfortunate. It's even perhaps unfair. And ultimately, find a way to make the best of it. To rise from the ashes and become better and stronger than ever before.

Road two: Being in denial. Questioning "Why me?" Focusing on how unfair it is, how everybody who hasn't had to experience what you have is just so damn lucky. Prioritising and identifying everything negative and how there's nothing good that comes from this.

And let me tell you, at the time, road two feels a much more natural, understanding road to take. I'd even go as far as to say it's the easier road. To blame, to deny, to surrender to the trauma and the change.

As I'm writing this, I'm imagining my twelve year old self unknowingly at this crossroads. On the verge of stepping down road two. I was in my hospital bed, feeling sorry for myself. I'd had another painful night, I could hardly move and it was so hot in the ward! Every minute seemed hard, life seemed hard. A week prior, I'd undergone a 20 hour life-saving liver transplant. This was a last resort to save my life after getting a rare liver disease called the Budd Chiari Syndrome. I was less than half my weight and I was unable to eat or even walk. I was suddenly days from death, in less than three months.

I'll always remember the conversation the liver specialists had with me when they told me a transplant was my only option. It was my best chance at living a normal life. Where I could go back to school, grow up and have a family. All of the things we normally take for granted.

But boy was I unaware of just how hard the recovery would be. I laid in that bed a week after the surgery and I just wanted to give up. It was too hard. I couldn't even sit up in bed. I was frustrated, tired and felt like I was the most unfortunate person who'd ever lived. I was defeated.

But after some stern "cruel to be kind" words from family and staff, I kept going. I was able to pull away and head down road one instead. My thoughts changed. I wasn't unlucky, hard-done-by or defeated. I was lucky to still be alive, and fortunate to have a second chance at life. The slate was wiped clean. Not only was I lucky to have been able to survive and now thrive, but I was lucky that I had help in heading down the right road.

Over the years I've come across many fellow transplant patients and others who've had traumatic health problems who sadly took the wrong road. Everything they did, said and thought was from the perspective of being defeated, being unlucky, being the most unfortunate person to have ever been born. I felt bad for them then and I still feel bad for them now.

I've been able to accept, embrace and transform my traumatic change into something positive and enlightening. I hold my hands up and say how lucky I was to go through everything I did. How I wouldn't have it any other way.

It's made me who I am today.

It's given me purpose, drive and a need to give back and hopefully help others to take the right road themselves.

My example might be a little extreme, but it's a lesson that can be applied to any and all negative changes. Minor to major, merely inconvenient to life-changing, we all face the same choice at the crossroads. It's important to remind ourselves of this choice often. Just because you took the right road once, doesn't mean you will again.

Since my experience at twelve years old, I've nearly died another two times at ages seventeen and twenty-nine. Both events were traumatic, painful, and scary. I had to work hard to catch myself when I would feel sorry for myself. I would try to use my situation as excuses to not be at my best, as reasons to be defeated, to hold my hands up and surrender.

Thankfully, I was able to make the right choice and take the right road every time. But it doesn't get easier, and you have to check yourself. I encourage you to find people who can support you during these times too—family, friends, peers. Likewise, we have to help guide others down the right road too.

When change comes, the only choice we have is to either make the most of it and find the positive, or to let it win and defeat us.

Fight Or Flight

Another way of looking at our choice when facing trauma and change is the age-old "fight or flight".

The choice between standing your ground and taking trauma and change head on… or running for the fields, defeated and lost. This is typically more associated with our mentality when facing our fears or psychological trauma. After years of trying, I think I've cracked the fight or flight formula and found a way of making sure fears and anxieties don't win.

Of course, we don't want to choose flight. Of course we don't want to run away. But when our thoughts, fears and anxieties are strong, it doesn't even feel like we have a choice in the matter. We just go for flight every time.

This, by the way, is the story of most of my life.

I've shared my physical health changes and trauma, but I've had my fair share of mental health challenges too.

Notice how I say fair share? In reality, it's probably not fair. But I'm making the conscious choice to accept, embrace and consider myself lucky for the changes and trauma!

Returning to school after my liver transplant and after a year of being away wasn't the triumphal return I had spent a long time imagining. After making my choice and focusing on the positive, I was so excited and felt lucky at the prospect of getting back to school. Of seeing my friends again. Of learning and growing.

Boy was I in for a shock when I returned (children and teenagers can be cruel)! And in a matter of a few weeks of being back at school, I went from being elated and feeling so fortunate to feeling very sad, anxious and unlucky.

Cruel words from the mouths of fellow students and even friends about my health experiences and my physical appearance post-trauma hit hard. Over time this transformed me into a socially anxious shell of a teenager with no self-confidence. I overthought everything, would wait for approval to speak and spent all of my free time thinking back on everything I'd done socially that day to pick out everything I did wrong.

I spiralled into depression, which massively limited my personal life, education and early career. Meanwhile, in my head, I was telling myself how much I hated myself for letting my mental state get this bad. I used to think that somebody else was better off having the life-saving liver transplant I had received because they would have made a better use of the second chance at life.

Less than a decade later, I had started my own business, went on to host webinars and speak on stage at events with over 500 people.

How? Well, I can tell you it wasn't bravery. I could have easily taken the flight option, time and time and time again.

But the reason I didn't was because of these two very key reasons:

First: I could help people. By sharing my stories, my marketing expertise, my knowledge, whether on stage, on webinars etc. I could help so many people and businesses. Thus giving back to the world that had saved my life. All I had to do was not let my anxiety beat me. When facing fight or flight, it's so so so easy to choose flight when you're the only one suffering. When others suffer as a result of taking that easy option, fighting feels much easier.

Two: I couldn't back out. I committed publicly to these scary actions months before they happened. I had people rooting for me. Friends, peers, family and my team. The prospect of backing out and running away, knowing that hundreds of people would know, was much scarier than just going and doing the scary thing in the first place!

To be clear, these methods haven't cured my anxieties. I'm still a shy, anxious and reserved person. And I think I always will be—it's who I am now. However, these two techniques have helped me to do the impossible.

Many people, including myself, never imagined I'd be speaking on stage to hundreds of people. And yet I did.

Whatever you fear, try to find ways of encompassing these two techniques to help make the flight option feel even scarier than fighting!

Oh, and by the way—remember how I used to hate myself for my anxieties and fear? I love the fact I have them now! They make me who I am, they allow me to be understanding of people and what they're going through, they allow me to help others, and they allow me to be very analytical which makes me a greater marketer. Because again, I've made the choice to accept, embrace and take the positive!

The School Of Life

You know the saying: "I went to the school of life" or "I went to the school of hard-knocks." For me, this very much rings true.

Whilst I was lucky enough to return to school after a year, it really did feel like a school of hard-knocks. Prior to my health problems, I was good at school. Close to top in most classes. Smashed my homework and coursework. Loved it.

A year of absence meant I had a lot to catch up with. Combined with other regular absences from appointments and getting ill every few weeks due to not having an immune system, I was constantly fighting to keep up.

Being the anxious student I had become meant I was easily distracted, too focused on those around me and found it hard to crack on.

I left school with *just* enough GCSEs to go to sixth form. A far cry from being top in most classes—but again, it's life!

Sixth form was the peak of my anxiety, which was aided by the very helpful head of the college who on my induction pointed my GCSEs out. The fact that I had scraped by made him assume that I wasn't a good student. As a result, he thought that I probably wouldn't get far in his college.

Two years later, I achieved A-levels just sufficient to gain admission to university.

University went better in terms of grades but the whole university experience was non-existent. Anxiety, combined with the fact I chose to go to university in my hometown, meant I wasn't on campus much. I went for lectures but also missed many out of fear. A room full of students and making presentations was a no-no. On top of this, in my second year, I spent some time in hospital recovering from nearly losing my transplanted liver.

But I focused on what I needed to learn for my assignments, and got a good grade. A year later, armed with my degree (which I honestly consider worthless now) and zero work experience, I managed to get my first job. Starting my marketing career eventually enabled me to start my own marketing agency.

It's been a tough and traumatic journey with many opportunities to quit, to give up, run and hide in a corner. But I subconsciously made the choice again to keep going and not give up.

When change and trauma finds its way to your door, it's important to give yourself time to accept it, overcome it and triumph. Because you'll always find a way. You just have to not take the road of despair.

Starting From Nothing

When I started my own marketing agency in 2019 it was very much another test of my anxiety, nerves and confidence. I made the leap from my safe, secure and well-paid marketing manager job to being completely self-employed—an action that everybody finds scary, yet I took the leap, armed with only two months worth of savings, a decade of marketing experience, and determination.

Why?

Simple maths really. I owe the world so much for saving my life three times. I crave giving back. The best way for me to do that is to use my marketing skills and knowledge to help businesses to grow and help their target audiences. By being employed, I was limited to helping one business and only a handful of people.

Now, I work with 50 businesses and 50 times the amount of people benefit. And it's only getting bigger.

I had selfish reasons too. I wanted to create the best life for me, my wife Kirsty (fiancé at the time) and our future family. We'd both been brought up with only the basics in life and I wanted to make sure our generation escaped the working class ways. Not gluttonous by any sense, just better off. With an income that meant we didn't have to worry about a rainy day or having to work until we were 80.

Oh and (between you and me), I can be quite stubborn and I always wanted to be my own boss so I couldn't be bossed around by anybody else!

So for all of these reasons, I'd thrown "common sense", nerves, anxiety and risk out of the window and went for it. And... I made it work! It wasn't easy. The first 12 months were some of the hardest of my life. Even now I face daily problems that simply wouldn't exist if I was still employed. But guess what? Like all of the other changes in my life, whilst this was by my choice, I wouldn't have it any other way.

I'm a stronger, better person because I took the leap. I contribute more to the world than ever before and make more money than I ever did in my previous day job. But... I also work far more hours than ever, have more sleepless nights than ever, have more costs than ever, have more stress and worries than ever.

So why wouldn't I change it for the world? Why do I have no regrets?

Because this is life, friends. Change breeds change, and it all comes back to that one choice we have. To embrace, accept and use it as a force for good. Or surrender, deny and let it beat us.

I would never endorse or recommend anybody quitting their career with two months worth of savings. It's so so so risky and I've been lucky to pull it off. But it's important to imagine where you can end up in life if you want to. Whether that's professionally or personally.

Your start in life... your upbringing... your physical and mental health challenges... None of this determines who you are and who you can become. That is up to you, and you alone.
In a world where you might not be able to trust in much... trust in yourself. You'll find a way to make it work.

Growing Or Dying

I often get told this is morbid but one of my most heartfelt and common sayings is: "If you're not growing, you're dying".

What do I mean? If you're not growing as a person, if you're not always learning, what's the point?

Growing and learning is life. And if you're not living, you're dying. This is another choice we all subconsciously make. As much as we like to think we do, we don't know it all. How can we? By being stubborn in our ways or ignorant of learning new things, we miss out on so much.

For me, this choice is a no brainer. It's obvious, a done deal. But again, I'm lucky. My experiences in life, my trauma, the change I've had to adapt to, has lined me up to be able to live in every sense of the word. And to boot, I even get called the human sponge because I'm constantly learning and absorbing!

This is another classic example of finding the positive in the negative. By accepting I don't know everything, that I always need to learn, and I'll never be the smartest person in the room… It means I'm a more understanding, open human being.

When clients invest significant funds in my marketing services, they know their results and returns will continue to improve. There's no ceiling.

So, What's The Point?

What is the point in choosing positivity over negativity when faced with changes and trauma? In choosing light over the dark. Hope over horror. Honestly, as I write this I struggle to fully explain it myself.

The choice has become so ingrained in me now that it doesn't feel like a choice. It's a compulsion, a desire, a fact. There is no real choice.

But I think it comes down to this: we can't always choose what happens to us. The changes we face. The trauma knocking at our door.

But we can choose how we deal with it and that really comes with a sense of power. A sense that life isn't all doom and gloom, as much as it may feel like it at the time. That we *do* ultimately have some say in what happens to us. That we are the ones in control. We call the shots. And you'll always find a way.

Trust yourself.

About Me

Hey I'm Dan, founder of Impactful Marketing and a Facebook Ads geek, trainer, speaker and author. When I'm not running my business and helping clients to grow theirs using Facebook Ads, I'm actively seeking ways of impacting the world for the better.

One way for me to achieve this is sharing my story of transforming trauma into triumph in this book. I have a debt to the world which I can never truly repay. By rights, I shouldn't even be alive! The NHS saved me three times.

Whilst I can never truly repay that, I'm doing everything I can to inspire, encourage and support others. We all face unexpected challenges, trauma and change. We shouldn't have to face them alone.

Impactful Marketing and my marketing knowledge are important vehicles to me giving back. By helping hundreds of businesses to grow and serve thousands of people, my impact is multiplying.

I dedicate my chapter, my learnings and my life to my beautiful wife Kirsty, our little-man Tristan, the NHS and the unknown gentleman who signed up as an organ donor and saved my life.

And remember; if you're not growing, you're dying!

From Developing Websites To Developing People

David Thorne
Founder and Lead Coach
David Thorne Ltd

"One cannot live the afternoon of life according to the program of life's morning; for what was great in the morning will be of little importance in the evening, and what in the morning was true will at evening have become a lie." – Carl Jung

This is the story of a chronically ill entrepreneur's midlife crisis. They went from developing websites to developing people. Someone who, mostly due to their genetic illness, listened more to the voice of ego than to that of genius. Who did as he was told, occasionally stepping over the line, transforming to being his true predominantly purple self. A web developer turned identity and self worth coach. In short, a part of my transformational journey.

During my forty-one years (at time of writing), I've had to rebuild my life due to failing health many times. These rebuilds have a remarkable similarity to many people's idea of a midlife crisis. While we may not exchange cars for super bikes, or leave a partner and start dating a far younger person, we have to adjust our working practices; maybe even stopping completely. We adjust our expectations, lower our "spoon count" and more, as our illness slowly deprives us of our humanity and ability to enjoy life. In short, we lose our ability to find and live our purpose.

You can be searching for your purpose for years. Some find it quickly, "I want to be an X, like mum or dad." Others think they know for years, "I love computers and enjoy programming so why not be a web developer?" – and yet, discover during their midlife crisis this isn't the case. There are also a few who search for most of their lives, maybe only finding it in their twilight years.

You can find yours in many ways. The easiest for many is to listen to that inner voice you have about what serves you and what doesn't. With practice you can learn to listen to that voice, identify which it is, and use it to your strengths. We all have multiple voices within us. Some are for protection, this is often defined as ego. Other voices are adventurous and creative. This voice is often referred to as genius. One is stronger than the other. Ask yourself now, which do you think you listen to more?

The L.A.B.E.L.S formula I use with many of my clients allows them to constantly assess what is serving them and what isn't, as well as helping them to keep moving towards their purpose. It was developed over many iterations of my life and only in the last four years or so has it become a part of my driving purpose.

L.A.B.E.L.S stands for

- Learn (what doesn't serve you)
- Accept (what you need to change)
- Believe (that change is possible)
- Experiment (with what fits you)
- Live (your new life)
- Stay (the course)

Learn What Serves You And What Doesn't

Today, I'm a successful entrepreneur who, despite my cystic fibrosis (CF), is running multiple businesses, including a web development shop and a growing coaching business where I coach people over thirty who feel lost and like they're running on autopilot, teaching them how to repair their relationships by redefining the stories that they tell themselves. This was done by using my L.A.B.E.L.S process, especially the Learn part.

For those who aren't aware, CF, the condition I was born with is a genetic condition affecting salt within the human body. This results in frequent chest infections, due to the lining of our lungs trapping bugs which typically pose no harm to humans due to their slow growth. In someone with CF, however, these same bugs are able to grow due to the mucus being so thick and trapping them in the lungs. This results in frequent chest infections and at present a life expectancy of about fifty years old. Back in 1983 when I was born, this life expectancy was between two and nine. We've always used two for me, due to the number of times I nearly died before then. This means as I write this (summer 2024), I am half way through my 21st lifetime as I see it.

In order to learn what serves us and what doesn't, a number of tools are available to you, including looking at which parts of life I enjoy, and which I don't. Of those that you don't, which are you able to let go of now (as opposed to later) and which do you really enjoy and want more of? This allows us to stay in higher vibration energy (where genius thrives). I have also competed at World Championships in Tang Soo Do (the Korean martial art I used to do) and generally lived life to the fullest. It's not always been like this though, if you'd been with me back in July 2017 you'd have found me in room 5, Princess Ward Papworth Hospital. My main source of company being that over bright fluorescent light, and familiar hospital smell, which for so many of you would inspire terror; for me a source of comfort.

I was in Papworth for a chest infection for my CF. I'd gone from being able to compete at martial arts World Championships, to barely being able to walk the five metres of the room I was in without needing to rest. My lung function was hovering at around 40%, a critical point for people with CF. 40% often marks an increase in deterioration in both quality of life and life expectancy. I was also in for "the talk". The talk varies from person to person. Typically it's that conversation you know you may have to have one day but really hope you never do. Your childhood pet has crossed the rainbow bridge. Your mum's on the phone, it's cancer and it's not looking good. That knock on the door from a police officer, "Can we come in please sir? It's about your wife..." For me that talk was transplant. Specifically a lung transplant. It should be made clear at this point that transplants are not cures for CF, they are simply swapping one serious set of medical problems for another. Every person with CF knows this talk may happen, yet dreads the day that it will. It should also be made clear that each transplant conversation happens at different points in a CF patient's life. When you have a history of depression like me, suicide attempts, or other mental health challenges, the conversation often starts earlier as the psychological assessment takes longer and is a higher priority. Conversations like this cause you to pause and reflect on your life, what you achieved and what you didn't. Many of us have been at a point where the pain just wasn't worth it. Sometimes we mean it, "I'm not doing that again." Or there's the hangover, "I'm never drinking again" knowing full well you will be by next Friday. You learn what you were doing won't work much longer.

There was a knock at the door. It was Dr Jones*. Stood there in their waistcoat looking serious as normal. They came in and sat on the bed. Now if you knew Dr Jones, you'd know this would rarely happen. In fact, I'd never known this to happen. By this point I'd been at Papworth for nearly twenty-three years. "David," they said, "...we need to talk about transplant."

The world stopped; a bustling and noisy ward no longer made a sound, the overly stuffy room suddenly felt chilly. It was like that scene in a movie where the lead character gets the news that defines the rest of the movie. The couple destined to be together meet across the crowded room, or the hero realises the ruler of the evil empire is in fact his dad. You could have heard a pin drop. Imagine how you would feel receiving this news. It was time for that dreaded conversation. My mother was visiting, "At least I now know how to silence David," she joked. It had one positive effect, it broke the tension!

In other words, change was coming for me whether I liked it or not. I'd learned what had been my life may not be any more. Massive doubt, imposter syndrome and more went through me. Along with a lot of fear, because let's face it, this was my life we were experimenting with.

Looking back now, I can see the entire L.A.B.E.L.S framework here in one short moment, although I admit, the belief part there and then would have been incredibly shaky!

Accept The Need To Change

Change was coming. As some of you will know, all change can be one of two things. A positive change or a negative one. This needed to be a positive change. After all, I wasn't forty yet, a number I really wanted to get to. It was the first major birthday of my dad and my mum which I remembered, and I liked the idea of being able to joke, despite CF, I'd made it to "the top of the hill". Without realising what had happened I had accepted I needed to change. Now to find out what that change would hold for me.

"But," Dr Jones added, with hope in their voice, "we also have to talk about Orkambi". Orkambi was a new drug, licenced, though not yet funded by the NHS. "I've some good news. As you're under 40% lung function now, you qualify for compassionate use." This is a scheme that allows for named patients in exceptional circumstances to be allowed to have the drug, even though the NHS isn't funding it. The cost is funded by the drug company, usually in exchange for further data in the hope of getting it approved for use by the NHS. This drug was performing miracles in the US. People on it were seeing great improvements in their quality of life and improvements in their lung function; something usually unheard of within CF.

I looked over at my mother, "What do we do?", suddenly feeling like a scared little boy again. "WE do nothing, it's your choice," she replied.

A debate ensued along with many technical questions. My distaste for excessive risk, fighting with my desire to survive. This is an example of ego protecting me, and genius being loud enough to be heard. For me, genius often invokes the spirit of Bushido (the Japanese "way of the warrior"). This battle raged for what felt like ages. The me that wanted everything versus the me that needed stability. I would eventually learn that the "stable me" was my ego fighting hard to protect me, to keep me in my comfort zone.

The me who wanted everything was my genius. It was screaming to be heard and listened to for once.

Later in life they would be assigned characters, my ego taking the role of an end of game "boss" from a computer game; tough and ruthless. Used to being in control. My genius is taking a split role hero of both a ninja and samurai, different characteristics "playable" at different times. A character design to protect others, and to explore and expand. People have done this before through time. "The devil and the angel on my shoulder"; or Jiminy Cricket in Pinocchio, your conscience.

In the end, it was decided I would try as I had very little to lose. The worst that would happen is in six months, we'd be having the same conversation, and at least I would know Orkambi hadn't worked.

Believe That You Can

A week or so later, having started the new drug, I started seeing changes. Whilst there was little to no improvement in my lung function (which never came; something I found out later wasn't that uncommon with Orkambi), I had more energy, and therefore was able to do more. "Use it or lose it" kept springing to mind. That as yet unnamed ninja kicked in, "Start now, or you'll never do it". My stubbornness kicked in, "Come on Thorne, what have you got to lose? Only your life!" Something I found both funny and scary at the same time. I should perhaps note here many people with chronic illnesses have an often very dark sense of humour. I refuse to be inauthentic in this chapter, dark humour and all.

I knew that the only way to overcome this lack of belief was to try to show I could do it. What I later would discover was known as "be the buffalo, not a cow". When a storm comes, the cow will back away, again and again until the storm covers them. This increases the length of time the storm is "in their lives" increasing the fear, the doubt and uncertainty they face. A buffalo takes the opposite approach. It walks into the storm, shortening the time it is in its mind. The quickest way through a storm is straight through. The Buffalo embodies this. The concept of this did come into my mindset through the martial arts training I had done, although I don't remember the analogy used, this was the approach I took. After all, if I did it, how could I not believe it could happen?

It's no different to that of Roger Bannister and the four-minute mile. Prior to him breaking it in 1954, it was believed impossible. By 1960, four others had done it. This brings me to my favourite technique, for overcoming challenges around belief. The Evidence Bag. It was taught to me by a fellow CF patient I will refer to simply by Kate. The Evidence Bag can be a physical bag as well as a memory bag. In it we place evidence of our achievements. Any achievement you make. Even if this is going as far back as learning to walk. It's not necessarily important to remember how you did it (although this helps) the importance is in *that* you did it.

When you put something in the Evidence Bag, you can then remember you did this thing the first time despite any beliefs to the contrary. So when you are at your first day at a job where you feel so out of depth, and questioning whether you can do it (regardless of whether you've been doing that role for years or not), you simply remember what you have in the Evidence Bag. "Ah yes I remember I also had the first day as a web developer working for the first time post university back in 2004…" It won't completely resolve any anxiety and tension you find, but it does help lessen it, often dramatically.

After all, nothing is quite as scary the second, third or fourth time around. I'd been using this for years without knowing what it was called, in fact I have several old lab books from my early web development days to this effect detailing how I did things. I've even googled things I know I've done before, and found my own blog article on how to do something. The Evidence Bag is a powerful ally in fighting imposter syndrome, anxiety over doing something (especially for the first time) and more. It's why it's a key tool I give to people early on when working with me.

Experiment With What Fits

With my Evidence bag in place, I decided to start with fitness, as many CFers are at their healthiest when they do regular exercise, especially with the right diet. I knew support and accountability was needed (not least as I always did best when being told what to do), so I found a specialist personal trainer, who had CF.

We started to work together online, improving my fitness. He also introduced me to the concept of mindset. This was something that I knew existed, you can't do over 10 years of martial arts and not be aware of it, though I had never really paid any attention to it. Especially the power it can have over all parts of your life. This reignited all questions, and desires from my martial arts days. A desire to fight, near enough, regardless of consequences to be the best that I could be arose in me. I like this to the ninja truly waking up.

Over the next three years I started investing more in myself, my mindset and training. I explored returning to full-time work over contracting, the old me desiring stability and the safety of a regular wage. Especially as I had just bought a new flat and moved out by myself again for the first time in six years. I searched for ways to grow my fledgling business so that it was a business rather than just a contracting role that would support me. Not all of these ideas worked out. At the time they felt like failures, only later did I realise that to FAIL was to Find An Important Lesson. And that the fear one feels when stretching outside of your comfort zone is simply False Evidence Appearing Real. Sometimes FEAR wins, and that's okay. Sometimes, the lesson you learn turns into the most powerful reason for doing what you do.

As Chloë Bisson, Founder of Inspired By Publishing and Co-Founder of Queens In Business, and co-author of this book often says, "Nothing is ever right, nothing is ever wrong, it just is." Your role is to find out what it is. And when you do, applying the principles within L.A.B.E.L.S, you will be able to respond to those challenges and questions which will arise, in a more positive manner and allow the changes that will come to improve your life far more than detract from it.

Live Your New Life

Things stabilised massively in my life, and there were many perceptions of improvements. I ended up with a great hybrid role for an Irish company (remote before remote was a thing) providing me with travel to Ireland, and a contract just long enough to give me the stability I craved. A new found love of weight lifting and chest infections dropping from seven to eight a year then one to two (indeed as I write this I've still not had eight chest infections and sets of intravenous antibiotics since 2017!).

I was also able to return to full time contracting (having seriously looked at adjusting to four, if not three days a week), and stay in my own flat, having worried for years that I wouldn't be able to keep it on without moving in with my non-existent partner.

Living your new life is a celebration of everything that you've achieved. For me this was actually just living a "normal" life. Paying the bills as best I could, approaching forty happy in the knowledge I would still be working, and new worries about this funny thing called a pension which I'd never previously bothered with as what are the chances of someone with CF working at fifty-six (at the time the minimum age to claim a private pension in the UK). Originally this was likely to be the end of L.A.B.E.L.S (without a name, and kept to myself) until I realised there was a further part, which complements Live very well.

Stay The Course

Then came 2020. We all know what happened in March. As someone with a chest based condition, this was an incredibly scary time. In August 2020 I ended up in hospital. Having recovered to upper 40% on Orkambi and Symkevi, (think version 1.5 of the drug) my lung function had more than halved to just over 20%. Dr Jones knocked at the door. This time seemingly dressed for surgery!

They came in and sat on the bed. Now you probably remember Dr Jones, and as such you know this would rarely happen. In fact, you can almost certainly see where this is going can't you? "David," they said "we need to talk about transplant." This time, there was no magic pill funded yet. The true successor to Orkambi (which was effective with 90% of the CF population world wide) received its licence and awaiting announcements of commencement of talks about licensing when we reached March. To the best of my knowledge talks hadn't gone further. It's hard to prevent FEAR kicking in at these points, especially when you're isolated and shut in a hospital room 24/7 with at least another two weeks to go. I called home and cried. Fear won that day. And that's okay.

The next day, a surprise announcement was made. Kaftrio (think version 2.0 of Orkambi) was approved for NHS use. This was a huge overnight change. Not only did Kaftrio work better than either of the previous treatments released, it was also able to be used by 90% of the CF population (Orkambi and the other version of the drug released was usable by 50% of the population at best). This was a game changer. This was my "last chance saloon".

Something, though, was stirring inside. This time there would be people who had never experienced Orkambi, or its "successor" Symkevi. They also had not necessarily ever learned how to live. They'd been too ill for too long. Something said "use it or lose it" and then I knew it was my job to help them learn how to live again (and in some cases for the first time). So true "use it or lose it" energy, although back in 2020 I didn't know why or what it would become I started again, and looked at what did or didn't serve me.

In 2023, whilst preparing something for a speech at the public speaking academy I am in, the phrase "go from developing websites to developing people" came to me, as well as the inspiration for L.A.B.E.L.S. A part of the end product of which you see in this chapter as I've continued to grow. Learning business properly, joining masterminds , studying property. I've found things that resonated and things that didn't. I learned that property didn't serve me as much as I would like. As such, I accepted this change didn't suit me (this is of course perfectly okay). I've studied public speaking, which I found I was naturally drawn to, as anyone who knows me will attest! And the inevitable midlife crisis change of looks, favouring a much more out there and edgy look, previous versions of me would never have dared show (although deeply wanted to).

I have expanded my comfort zone so far that 2020 Dave wouldn't recognise me, let alone twelve year old David (who disliked the name Dave). I try to stretch that comfort zone every day, as I strive to be among the first people with CF to reach 100 years old! I hope that learning skills like L.A.B.E.L.S, and the Evidence Bag can help you to start to grow too.

**Names have been changed to protect the identities of Drs at Papworth Hospital's general request.*

About Me

Hi I'm Dave and I am an Identity and Self Worth Coach, who is also known as The Stigma Coach. I specialise in coaching over 30s to achieve their midlife dreams without the midlife crisis. I also coach the chronically ill, disabled and neurodiverse to overcome the daily stigma they face.

I'm an Emotional Change Therapist, intuitive coach and public speaker who has appeared in Queens In Business magazine and now co-author in the first Queens In Business Book to feature men. I also have Cystic Fibrosis, which could have limited my life far more than it has, thanks to the training I have done, and now teach others to do.

Born in Manchester, but growing up mostly in East Anglia, school was a mixed blessing. I was unwell and in hospital semi-frequently so I didn't learn social skills in the traditional way of playgroups and nursery. As such, later in school I was often bullied, and feeling out of place. A love of martial arts helped combat some of this and founded the basis of the mindset I developed. It wasn't until my mid thirties when I started to deal with the issues I faced that I discovered my calling. And even then it was only because I was facing that "cliff edge" that I wasn't willing to be shoved over.

I want to dedicate this chapter to Julia, Emily, and Christian Lyons of Ontario Canada. Julia and Christian have Cystic Fibrosis (Julia sadly passed in 2011). Julia inspired her sister Emily into entrepreneurship and, in turn, Emily reinvigorated my entrepreneurial desires when running my own business due to my health seemed hopeless. Her brother Christian also runs his own small businesses. This dedication is just a small thank you to Julia and Christian who I can never meet, but inspire me to live my life to the fullest, and be the best entrepreneur with CF that I can be. As well as Emily who inspires me more than I can ever truly express.

Fear To Success To Fear Again

Andy Nisevic
Managing Director
One Degree Training and Coaching

"I learned that courage was not the absence of fear, but the triumph over it. The brave man is not he who does not feel afraid, but he who conquers that fear." – Nelson Mandela

I don't know about you but I hate writing these intros. It feels like writing a lonely heart entry or dating app entry to be all 21st century about it! I'll give it my best shot though.

I'm Andy Nisevic. First and foremost, I'm a very proud dad. I wish I could write husband or partner and dad, but life hasn't taken me on that path.

I became a dad quite young at twenty-three. The beauty of which is that in my *almost* (this is important to emphasise!) mid-forties, I have a grown up daughter, Amelia, who I have some similar interests to. This also means that we enjoy doing stuff together, and I'll still be young enough to be a fun grandad, if and when the time comes.

When I first started my business and people would ask me who I am, my first reaction was to tell them my name and what I do. As though what I do somehow defines who I am as a person. It definitely forms part of my identity, but only that—a part. The biggest part of my identity is being the dad that I am. I can't claim to be perfect, I only have one daughter, and got bloody lucky with her.

I'm also an absolute geek when it comes to human behaviour, human psychology, and the psychology of leadership. Inside of work, I've seen a good deal of success. The fascination I have for psychology, especially leadership psychology, led me to who I am in a professional context. I'm a self-employed leadership trainer, mentor, coach and author.

Outside of work, I've struggled. Although I've always had a fantastic relationship with my daughter, I've spent the vast majority of my life alone. I often considered success as holistic, you're either successful or you're not. My life outside of work was certainly not.

Where It All Began

I spent 23 years in the Royal Air Force. I was a successful non-commissioned officer; I left as a flight sergeant with an offer of promotion to warrant officer, which is the highest non-commissioned rank there is. The final role I held in the RAF was teaching their leadership and management courses. It was here that my interest in human behaviour transitioned into full on geekery.

I was fortunate enough throughout my career to have been promoted three times (with an offer of a fourth that I turned down). At each promotion, it's RAF policy that you attend leadership training appropriate to your new rank. I loved the courses, they were fun, engaging, informative, taught well, and interesting. They didn't make me a good leader though. That's something that I can admit with the benefits of hindsight, experience, and knowledge. I would not have admitted it at the time.

It was teaching the RAF's leadership courses and hearing so many horrible stories of such terrible leadership (provided by people who'd attended these excellent courses), that made me reflect on myself.

I can say with full honesty, that I always had good intent. I wanted to be liked, I didn't want to be the "toxic leader" that so many people talk about. The truth is that I was a great leader, for some people. To those who responded well to my natural style of leadership. To those who didn't respond well, I was a terrible leader.

It was this realisation, that you can be a great leader, and a terrible one, all at the same time, that made me want to do things differently.

When I made the decision to leave the RAF, I had no intentions of starting my own business. The idea that I, some kid from a council estate who struggled to build relationships outside of my immediate workplace, could be seen as a managing director just didn't seem right.

I had this self-perception that had actually kept me in the RAF for as long as I'd stayed. Being in the RAF wasn't easy, but it was safe. I knew what I was doing, I knew I had a wage coming in, my pension was building, I had free health and dental care and free access to gyms and fitness classes. Plus, as long as I was in, I'd never be homeless.

The truth was, that I'd wanted to leave the RAF for about a decade before I actually did. Many postings, many deployments, and many missed experiences with my daughter made me feel as though I should be doing something else. All those postings and deployments, also meant that I never managed to build relationships with people outside of my direct workplace. I'd met women, and had short-term relationships, but the constant moving meant I never spent anywhere long enough to build the foundations needed for a long-lasting relationship.

I wanted to leave, I just didn't see myself able to do anything else. I didn't believe I was capable, outside of the military, of having a career or earning what I needed to pay the mortgage, support my daughter Amelia, and have enough left to have a life.

That self-belief, or lack thereof, kept me stuck in a job and way of life, that made me miserable.

How Things Changed

In 2020, apart from the obvious that was going on in the world, the unit I was part of in Lincolnshire was being moved to Northumberland. The RAF station we were moving to was in a beautiful part of the world, roughly halfway between Newcastle and the Scottish borders.

I'd served there before, and knew just how hard it was to maintain my relationship with my daughter from there. Her mum and I split in early 2006, when Amelia was two. Later that year, her mum, who was in the RAF as well, was moved to Lincolnshire. As a Corporal, having recently started a new role there, I was in no position to move to be closer to them. This meant that for around three years, I drove 200 miles to collect her, and another 100 miles to my closest family members (my mum's) for somewhere to stay to ensure I saw my daughter every fortnight.

Every other weekend was a 600-mile round trip to see her. Not only that, I had to pass up social events and potential relationships so I had the time and money to not only see Amelia but entertain her too.

Three years of doing that left me tired. Not miserable, or even unhappy, because, if I had to, I'd do it all over again. But I was tired. I was also lonely. There are only so many social functions you can turn down before people stop asking.

I just had no desire to accept that as my fate, without finding something else.

As someone who'd had an interest in leadership, stemming from my own good and bad experiences, and as someone with years and years of experience as a trainer, I looked into leadership training for the RAF. Initially I looked at officer training. It was based in Lincolnshire too, so there'd be no need to move. After visiting though, I knew it wasn't for me. Their routine included many weekends, and late nights. My priority was to maintain contact with my daughter and that role would've made it incredibly difficult.

I then saw posts being advertised at the Airman Command Squadron, the unit that provides leadership training for non-commissioned officers. Although it was more than 100 miles away, the working routine was Monday to Friday, 8am-5pm. I'd actually see more of Amelia by moving there than I would staying local and teaching at officer training. I successfully applied and it was the best move I made.

I thoroughly enjoyed everything about the role. What we taught, the way we were taught to teach it, how it was taught, and the freedom we were given to bring the training to life in creative ways. I knew I'd found something that I'd happily do for the rest of my life. The problem was, because it was what's known as an "out of trade job", I could only do it for three years before having to go back to the operational job.

I researched development courses to improve my facilitation skills, and enrolled on a professional coaching diploma. I became a volunteer facilitator for a charity who supports veterans who've experienced mental health difficulties to start seeing their future in a more positive light.

Through the coaching training, I saw the many different jobs and ways of earning a living that I'd never heard of, or considered. My mind opened to many other possibilities, and I started to realise that there could be something for me outside of the RAF.

As a volunteer, I began applying what I was helping other people with to myself, and realised that if I was being honest with myself, I was my own worst enemy. I was keeping myself tied to the RAF, because I didn't believe I had anything else to offer. I was trapping myself in a life that didn't make me happy.

There was an important realisation that I had on this shift in thinking. Many people over the years had told me things like, "I don't give myself enough credit" or "there's no reason why I couldn't be successful outside the RAF". While I appreciated the sentiment behind being told things like that, I never actually believed them. I carried on in the same way I always had.

By attending these courses, facilitating training on overcoming limiting beliefs, etc, I came to the realisation myself. This meant the arguments I had previously used to counter the points made by other people were much, much, quieter. Realising it myself made it so much more believable.

While there was no deliberate tactic I employed, or investment that I made to change my mindset, the exposure to people who think differently to the way I always had created a shift in my own thought processes.

Learning on the coaching diploma, coupled with the volunteer work I did, layered with my own reading of psychology, mindset, and leadership psychology, really made me question why I was persisting in a career in the RAF when I really wasn't happy.

As I approached the final six months of my three-year tour as a leadership trainer, I began looking at other options. I'd been offered promotion to Warrant Officer, which is a highly paid, highly influential rank. I was looking at the options available, not only were they nowhere near where I wanted to live, the prospect of doing those jobs for the next X number of years made me miserable.

I made the decision to leave on a Monday, which was day four of the four-day course I volunteered on. By the end of the next day, I'd not only told my boss that I was going to leave, I'd submitted my notice on the system. My fingers were trembling as I went through the process. My heart was pounding. I'll admit, I almost chickened out. As soon as I pressed submit though, I had a big beaming smile, bigger than I'd had in years.

I applied for many roles as a leadership trainer for these companies. Some turned me down, three were offered to me.

They were for large corporate training providers and very well-paid jobs. They all had the same approach. A standard slide pack, standard script, predominantly online, and a "branded" way of providing the training.

One of the ladies I met on the coaching diploma invited me to a free training day with a firm who mentored entrepreneurs. The idea of starting my own business hadn't yet occurred to me, but I thought, "it's free, why not?!"

This was the biggest turning point. The delivery of the training made me realise that actually running a business was very similar to running an operational campaign. You had strategic outcomes, milestones, and tactics. The only difference was that I would be the one setting those objectives, and determining the tactics, rather than just carrying them out.

I realised that I was doing the same thing I'd always done. Playing it safe. These corporate training providers didn't meet my values; I knew the end product. The person who'd completed the training was less important than the number of people put through the training. Those jobs would've been a safe salary, not something that would leave me feeling fulfilled.

This realisation planted the seed to start my own business. I'd theorised why, despite such good training being available out there, there were still far too many examples of such poor leadership. I believed I had the answer to a huge problem in the working world, I just had no idea where to start or how to value my service.

After seeking out both free and paid for training, I attended a two-day business strategy conference. It was here that I met someone who would later become my first mentor in business, and he scared the bejeebers out of me! I'd attended some training that suggested you price your services using a very simple formula—how much money you'd like to make, divided by the number of people you'd like to work with. This formula led to me believing that my twelve-month programme would be worth £3,500. The chap I met told me I needed to quadruple those fees immediately!

Suddenly I went from someone who could earn £70k per year (far more money than I'd ever earned in a single year before) to someone potentially sitting on a multi six-figure business.

Don't Discount The Little Things

I'm not going to claim that I'm someone who doesn't care about money. I like having money in both my pocket and my bank account. I like the safety and security of having it. I also like to spend it and enjoy myself. But the idea that I, some kid from a council estate who left school with nothing of note to his name, who joined the military because he couldn't afford a place of his own, who stayed because he didn't believe he could do anything else, could now have a business where he could earn a six-figure salary, was just barmy.

The event was in London, I live in Lincoln, and I cry-laughed the entire drive home. I knew I wanted it. It wasn't the potential quarter of a million pound revenue I could generate. It was the fact that I now realised how much playing it safe was holding me back. I wasn't someone who was limited to a £50k a year salary (which is still a great salary). I also wasn't someone who was limited to a business that would max out at £70k per year, which, after expenses, would've allowed me to pay myself roughly the same salary as I would've had in the RAF or at one of the corporate jobs, especially after the RAF pension had been applied. I was someone who had something substantial to offer the world. Something with real value, that would make a real difference. That something was me.

I jumped in. I turned down the offer of promotion. I turned down the three job offers. I cancelled the progress of all the other job applications I had in motion. I registered my business and started networking. I worked full time in the business from 10th October 2022, and by 31st August 2023, I'd generated my first £100k in revenue.

Here's the big realisation I've had in the journey. There is no one thing that's going to make a difference. It's not one coach, or one experience, or one realisation that's suddenly going to give you a completely different outlook on life. There are plenty of examples that I've given in this chapter where I felt as though I was a new man, with a new outlook. The truth is that they all helped, but individually, all they did was give me a new perspective. But I still behaved in the same way.

For example, leaving the safety of the RAF (which made me miserable) to the safety of a corporate job (which would have made me miserable), to hugely undervaluing my services (which would have meant I'd have to max myself out just to earn a safe wage).

The important thing isn't to look out for one thing that's going to make a difference. It's to look out for the little things, and be open to them making a small change in perspective. On reflection, there were loads of times throughout my life that, had I been more open to change and not been ruled by fear, I could've had a very different life, with many different experiences. I was convinced that I needed something big to happen to me to transform my life. So I closed myself off to the little things that end up having a compound effect. Had I met the chap who went on to become my first mentor, without having gone through the mini-mindset shifts, I probably would've laughed at him and walked away.

It Doesn't End

I want to be clear, I haven't earned anywhere near a quarter of a million pounds in revenue. But there is the potential, and I'm working towards it. Year one capped off at £120k, which allowed me to make several big and expensive investments in myself and the business. I didn't make a profit in year one, because I spent BIG.

There's some deep psychology behind spending money, especially when you make it far faster than you've ever had it before. There are lots of studies online that say between 35% and 70% of lottery winners end up broke.

Although year one from a business perspective was very successful, I personally didn't make much money. It's not wasted, they're investments that will pay off in the long run. If I'm honest with myself though, with the benefit of hindsight, there were better investments that would've secured the foundations of my fledgling business, rather than rushing to reach the next level.

I went from someone who always played it safe to someone who took risks.

I believe that my past resistance to doing anything that would make things better for me, and the amount of time I spent miserable because of it, resulted in a huge over-correction.

Having £120k worth of clients sounds great, and it is, but they now need serving. It's one thing to get the business; it's something very different to get the business, serve the clients, and still keep new business trickling in.

I'm over halfway through year two and have barely made 20% of what I made in year one. Despite my social media audience, my position of authority, my reputation all being very positive, year two has been very different.

There are a number of factors behind this, but ultimately I tried to become someone different to who I naturally am. I'm a naturally cautious person. I used that caution to keep myself trapped because I used it to close myself off to opportunity. Taking a chance on myself led to quick success, but led me to throwing caution to the wind. As I write this chapter, the reality is that I'm six weeks from my business failing.

That's why I've called this chapter Fear To Success To Fear Again, because it was fear that held me back in the past, but taking too many risks has led me to a point where I'm scared again.

The big "so what" for any reader to take away is that life needs to have balance.

Yes, we need to be open to the small things that will make a small difference. Those small differences will have a compound effect and take you on a journey. But when you're not true to who you naturally are, that initial excitement wears off.

In September 2023, I told myself that I need to invest in bringing in someone to help me with business development. I told myself that I was reverting to old habits and not trusting myself. I convinced myself that I'd proven that I was capable of being successful because I'd take less than a year to earn six-figures. That was true, I was capable of doing it. There's a reason why successful CEOs and businesses have personal and/or executive assistants. There's a reason why companies outsource various services. Because when you're doing it alone, you're doing it wrong. I tried to do it alone, and it put me straight back into fear again.

Recognise what you're not good at and as soon as you're able, find someone to do that for you. Whether it's outsourced or a permanent hire will depend on many factors, the important thing is to recognise is the right support at the right time.

About Me

I am a leadership specialist, number 1 best-selling author of Leadership 101: Don't be a Dick, keynote speaker, and veteran of twenty-three years in the RAF.

Since leaving the RAF, I combined my passion for helping people with my extensive knowledge of leadership to create coaching and training programmes that help managers become great leaders. Over the years, I was lucky enough to work with some fantastic leaders, I also worked for some terrible ones. I was also both a great and terrible leader – sometimes both at the same time!

Harnessing both the highs and lows of my experiences, I blended them with scholarly theories and psychological principles, and curated a range of innovative workshops and masterclasses. My purpose is simple: to make the workplace a more fulfilling and engaging place, so the business, and people within them, thrive.

Adapt To Change

Rebecca Tsang Mang Kin
Entrepreneur and Change Management Consultant
Athos Relocation

"If you want something you've never had, you must be willing to do something you've never done." – Thomas Jefferson

My name is Rebecca, and my life has been a vibrant tapestry of continuous adaptation and transformation. Imagine a young girl on the sun-drenched island of Mauritius, driven by an insatiable thirst for knowledge and curiosity as boundless as the ocean surrounding her. That girl was me, always eager to discover what lay beyond the horizon.

In Mauritius, I completed the French Baccalaureate with a focus on sciences. Despite average results, my determination to seek higher education abroad remained unwavering. This led me to Leeds, where I undertook a foundation course, preparing for A-level exams in English, Maths, and Economics. The transition was a whirlwind, challenging me academically and linguistically as I shifted from thinking in French to mastering English.

My journey continued to Manchester, where I pursued a BSc in Management and Marketing of Textiles. After my undergraduate degree, I ventured into Computing Science at Imperial College. However, the extensive hours on the computer led to repetitive strain injuries, prompting another pivotal shift – this time towards law.

I completed a Postgraduate Diploma in Law (PGDL) and the Bar Vocational Course (BVC), a path offering the flexibility I craved. This qualification allowed me to practise as a barrister, recognised back home in Mauritius. If I returned to Mauritius, I could seamlessly become a barrister, and if I stayed in the UK, I could work as a paralegal before converting to a solicitor.

Several years as a paralegal and litigation solicitor in London preceded my return to Mauritius after marriage. Back home, I worked for my family business while studying for the notary exam and completing my barrister qualification through pupillage. The notary exam in Mauritius is particularly challenging, and the profession highly exclusive, with limited notaries. To ensure a viable career path, I pursued my barrister qualification alongside my notary studies.

Starting my own business in the UK was an entirely different challenge. Without a network or funding, I had to do everything myself. Despite the challenges, I held fast to my vision, understanding that long-term success would require delegation and subcontracting. Many advised me to focus, suggesting I was trying to do too much at once. Yet, I believe that with a clear vision and enough people believing in it, anything is achievable. The power of collaboration is immense.

Today, I wear many hats. I am an entrepreneur with multiple ventures, including a relocation and letting business, mediation, and legal consultancy. I am also a utilities partner with Utility Warehouse and Fidelity Energy. Additionally, I am working on launching a podcast and this collaborative book on adapting to change.

On a personal note, I am a daughter, wife, mother, friend, and businessperson. My core values of integrity and authenticity guide me in every aspect of my life and work. A significant mindset shift I have adopted is realising that time is more precious than money and that solving people's problems is what truly matters.

Overcoming Doubts

Before embarking on my entrepreneurial journey, I spent nine years in Mauritius working for my family's retail businesses. Life seemed idyllic with the comforts of a big house and maids, yet beneath the surface, my husband's discontentment prompted a significant change.

We relocated to Reading, a place where we knew no one apart from my immediate family – my husband and son. Although I had some relatives nearby in Binfield and cousins and an aunt in London, none were able to help me start my own business. This lack of a local network compounded my self-doubt.

Initially, I believed my only option was to return to the legal field as a solicitor in litigation. This belief was so strong that I immediately asked my former boss for a job upon arriving in Reading. He agreed, but as the time approached, his enthusiasm waned, and I, too, had second thoughts. Returning to a traditional job felt like trading my freedom for short-term financial stability.

Determined to find a new path, I embraced flexibility and completed an intensive five-day course to become a mediator. This new skill opened doors, but my passion for property investment remained. Attending seminars and talks dispelled the myth that substantial capital was needed to start in property.

Faced with another crucial decision, I had to choose between focusing on mediation or property relocation. After much deliberation, I chose property relocation, realising the importance of a clear, singular message on social media.

Throughout my journey, my mindset was a significant hurdle. I often felt too old to learn new skills and was intimidated by networking and self-promotion. The fear of rejection and failure were constant companions. However, by acknowledging these fears and actively working to overcome them, I discovered the truth in Zig Ziglar's words: "You don't have to be great to start, but you have to start to be great."

Through perseverance and adaptability, I learned that one is never defined by a single identity. Today, I am more focused on my goals, and each challenging step has been instrumental in shaping who I am.

Change is Constant

Life has been a series of transformations, each bringing its own set of challenges and opportunities. Moving from Mauritius to England was one of the most significant changes in my life. Transitioning from thinking and speaking in French to mastering English was a major cultural shift. University life in Leeds introduced me to a new culture and academic environment, setting the stage for my future adaptability.

Professionally, my career began in London as a personal assistant, then as a paralegal, and eventually as a solicitor. However, a pivotal moment came when I moved back to Mauritius to take on a leadership role in my family business. This shift from employee to boss was comfortable and fulfilling but also the precursor to my next major change.

Returning to the UK, specifically to Reading, marked the start of a completely new chapter. Unlike my previous experience, this move involved finding a home, adjusting to a new community, and starting from scratch professionally. Downsizing from a four-bedroom house to a two-bedroom apartment was challenging, but we embraced it as part of our new journey. Finding the right school for my son was a primary concern, involving extensive research to identify the best suitable school for my son.

The move to Reading was not just about physical relocation; It was a profound professional shift as well. Starting my business in a new environment without a local network was daunting. Initially, I leaned on my legal background and sought to return to my previous employer. However, this plan didn't materialise as expected, and I soon realised that returning to a traditional legal role would limit my potential and freedom.

Instead, I ventured into mediation, taking a five-day intensive course to become a certified mediator. Despite this achievement, my passion for property investment remained. Attending seminars and networking events changed my perception that substantial capital was needed to start. Focusing on property relocation required clear marketing and a singular message on social media, which led me to prioritise this over mediation.

Joining Business Network International (BNI) was another pivotal moment. Through daily pitching and meeting new people, I refined my business model and expanded my network. I quickly became a Green Club member within nine months, significantly boosting my confidence and business prospects. I realised the potential of collaboration over competition, leading to partnerships that enhanced my service offerings. This shift allowed me to build relationships with letting agents, landlords and corporate clients, securing contracts to relocate employees of large corporations such as Procter & Gamble.

A significant personal change was adopting a growth mindset. The pressure to become financially independent in a new environment was immense. Investing in personal development, attending courses, and listening to podcasts transformed my approach. Books like "Who Not How" by Dan Sullivan and "Start Now Get Perfect Later" by Rob Moore played a crucial role in changing my perspective on business and collaboration. As Buddha said, "There is no path to happiness. Happiness is the path."

By focusing on who can help rather than how to do everything myself, I embraced the power of collaboration and subcontracting. This approach reduced the need for employees and allowed me to leverage the expertise of others, enhancing the quality and scope of my services.

Having an open mind and the willingness to learn have been crucial. I did several courses, training, and invested heavily in personal development. However, ultimately, action is what matters. Sometimes unexpected opportunities arise, and it's up to you to seize them. For example, joining Utility Warehouse and Fidelity Energy was not planned, but through networking, I saw the value in integrating these into my business.

Overall, my journey has been marked by continuous learning and adaptation. Each change, whether personal or professional, has shaped me into a resilient and resourceful individual, constantly evolving to meet new challenges and seize new opportunities. Embracing change is also about discovering who you are. By adapting to change, I had to know who I am, what my values are, and what is important to me so I can work towards it.

Today, I find myself in a remarkable position, having relocated to Reading with a crystal-clear vision of my goals, both personally and professionally. As a distinguished solicitor of England and Wales, a barrister in Mauritius, and a qualified mediator, I am well-equipped to face any challenges that come my way. My entrepreneurial spirit thrives through several businesses, including a property investment business, a relocation service, and efforts to build my personal brand as a recognised authority in the field. Upcoming ventures like launching a podcast and co-authoring a book with Chloë Bisson mark exciting new chapters in my journey.

The management of my rental properties in London and Mauritius, along with my role on the board of directors for my family's business, reflects a balanced blend of personal initiative and family commitment. My personal life, too, mirrors this harmony, with my husband finding his own purpose and my son's recent admission to a prestigious private secondary school.

Embracing Changes

Change is a constant in life, yet many people fear it, craving the comfort of the familiar. I was no different. Before moving from Mauritius to Reading, I questioned my motives, wondering if I was ungrateful for my life in Mauritius. But no place is perfect, and each has its own challenges and opportunities.

Experience taught me that fighting change is futile. Despite my love for planning and control, life's unpredictability made me realise that embracing change was essential. As Marcus Aurelius said, "The happiness of your life depends upon the quality of your thoughts." I learned to focus on what I could control and let go of the rest.

To start embracing change, I tackled small, manageable tasks to build my confidence. Inspired by James Clear's "Atomic Habits," I adopted the principle of making tiny changes to create remarkable results. Gradually, I became more adept at handling larger challenges. Jason Osborne helped me see that worrying about uncontrollable factors was counterproductive. His advice to focus on actionable steps transformed my approach.

For instance, I was stressed about refinancing my property. Jason's guidance helped me concentrate on what I could control, significantly reducing my anxiety. This shift in mindset, aligned with the idea of focusing on small, consistent improvements, was transformative, enabling me to act decisively and effectively.

Embracing discomfort has been crucial. Tackling small tasks and gradually facing bigger ones has made me more resilient.

Meditation has also helped me maintain focus and manage stress.

A poignant moment was when my young son, seeing my distress, encouraged me with, "Mum, you always tell me to try my best and not give up. You can do this." His words reminded me of the strength and resilience I needed to embody for both of us.

Today, I embrace change and uncertainty. As James Norbury said, "Fear will not stop you from dying, but it may stop you from living." And Winston Churchill wisely noted, "The pessimist sees difficulty in every opportunity; the optimist sees the opportunity in every difficulty."

Lessons In Gratitude, Growth And Networking

One of my greatest lessons has been understanding the power of gratitude and recognising that even small wins matter. Through networking and engaging with diverse people, I've encountered many individuals who overcame great challenges to achieve success. Their compelling reasons – their "why" – pushed them to persevere and never give up on their dreams.

From these interactions, and reinforced by reading "The Gap and the Gain" by Dan Sullivan and Dr. Benjamin Hardy, I learned not to compare myself to others but to measure my progress against my past self. This shift in perspective has taught me to appreciate my achievements for what they are and to be content with my journey. Instead of feeling jealous of others' successes, I focus on my growth and accomplishments, profoundly changing my mindset.

I now see opportunities everywhere and have developed a love for connecting people. This perspective has been transformative both personally and professionally. Attending numerous networking events and meeting a wide array of individuals has allowed me to build a robust network. However, I've learned that building a network takes time and that the true value lies in the relationships you cultivate and the help you provide to others. Maya Angelou's words resonate deeply with me: "People will forget what you said, people will forget what you did, but people will never forget how you made them feel."

Networking is not just about expanding your contacts; it's about fostering genuine connections and being willing to help others succeed. This approach has not only grown my network but has also broadened my perspective, leading to new insights and opportunities for my business. By focusing on helping people and understanding their needs, you can develop a supportive network that enhances your own growth as well.

Another important lesson is valuing myself and my expertise. Despite my numerous qualifications, I struggled to feel confident about my value. This discomfort often made me reluctant to charge clients appropriately for my services. The story of Picasso and a napkin sketch resonated deeply with me:

Picasso was once enjoying a drink at a café when someone recognised him and asked for a quick sketch on a napkin. Picasso obliged and then asked for a surprisingly high price. The person was shocked, arguing it only took a few minutes. Picasso famously replied, "It didn't take minutes, it took a lifetime to be able to draw this in minutes." This story highlights the value of an artist's experience and skill, which goes beyond the time spent creating a single piece.

This narrative helped me understand the worth of my education and legal expertise. It took years of hard work and dedication to reach the level where I could effectively help people with their legal and financial problems. Recognising this value has been crucial in my journey.

In litigation, I've also learned to assess the true cost of fighting a legal battle. Often, clients claim they are fighting for principles, but litigation is primarily about money. It is essential to consider the time, energy, and financial resources required to pursue a case. Winning a case for a large sum of money is meaningless if the opposing party cannot pay. This insight has guided me to advise clients pragmatically, focusing on outcomes that truly benefit them.

I have also changed how I handle mistakes and frustrations. Previously, I would get angry and upset when others' errors caused me losses. Now, I approach these situations more calmly. Depending on the situation, I either express my dissatisfaction and move on, or I collaborate with the person to find a solution. Shouting and blaming do not resolve issues; constructive communication does.

Adopting the mindset, "If you think you can, you can. If you think you can't, you can't. Both are right," has been transformative. It underscores the power of belief in shaping outcomes. Embracing a positive mindset has allowed me to navigate challenges more effectively and continue growing both personally and professionally.

Overcoming Limiting Beliefs and Building a Resilient Mindset

Addressing my limiting beliefs and building a resilient mindset has been transformative. Initially, my fears of failure, rejection, and the unknown often led to self-doubt. I struggled with the belief that I wasn't good enough or qualified, which further hindered my progress.

To overcome these limiting beliefs, I focused on small, manageable tasks. By achieving small successes, I gradually built confidence. Each accomplishment reinforced my abilities and reduced my fear of failure, enabling me to tackle larger challenges.

A pivotal moment was realising that worrying about things outside my control was unproductive. Jason Osborne advised me to concentrate on what I could control, shifting my focus to actionable steps. This insight empowered me and reduced feelings of overwhelm.

Investing in personal development was crucial. Engaging in courses, podcasts, and books offered new perspectives and strategies. "The Gap and the Gain" by Dan Sullivan and Dr. Benjamin Hardy taught me to compare my progress to my past self, fostering a positive mindset. "Go for No" by Richard Fenton and Andrea Waltz reframed my perception of failure, teaching me that each "no" brings me closer to a "yes."

Networking through Business Network International (BNI) and several networking events played a significant role. Meeting diverse people who overcame adversity reinforced the importance of having a strong "why" to stay motivated. Within nine months, I became a Green Club member, boosting my confidence and expanding my professional network.

Embracing discomfort was essential. Challenging myself and stepping out of my comfort zone helped me adapt to new situations. Adopting the motto "FAIL" (First Attempt In Learning) reframed failure as a stepping stone to success.

Mentorship from Adam Wickes was instrumental. Adam provided invaluable advice and helped me think differently. For example, when I was focused on unnecessary details for my property investment, he advised me to secure an investor first and worry about systems later. This practical advice realigned my priorities.

Maintaining a mindset of gratitude and positive thinking has been transformative. Celebrating small wins and appreciating progress, no matter how incremental, kept me motivated and resilient. Neville Wright's story of overcoming ADHD, dyslexia, and poverty to achieve success was particularly inspirational. He emphasised, "Without action, there is nothing. All the talking, reading, and planning come to nothing if not followed by implementation. Now." His story reinforced the importance of immediate action and flexibility.

Nick James' philosophy of transitioning from "life is not fair" to "I am responsible and take action" resonated deeply. He highlighted that managing your mental and emotional state is the greatest skill in business and life. Adopting a structured approach and maintaining discipline has been critical. As Nick James said, "Absence of structure is what makes you overwhelmed."

Robin Sharma's insights from "The 5 AM Club" also played a key role. He reminds us that "excuses are seducers, fears are liars, and doubts are thieves." This perspective helped me overcome self-doubt and embrace challenges as opportunities for growth. His words, "The truth is that every challenging event you've experienced, each toxic person you've encountered, and all the trials you've endured have been the perfect preparation to make you into the person you are now," have been a source of strength.

Advice To My Younger Self

If I could give my younger self one piece of advice about growth and change, it would be to embrace change and not let fear hold you back. Fear of failure can be paralysing, but it is also one of the greatest teachers. Every failure is an opportunity to learn and grow.

Change is inevitable, and resisting it only makes the process more difficult. Instead of fearing the unknown, see it as a chance to explore new possibilities and develop new skills. Step out of your comfort zone, because that's where real growth happens.

It's okay to make mistakes. Each misstep is just a "First Attempt In Learning" (FAIL). Don’t let the fear of failing prevent you from pursuing your dreams. You are more resilient and capable than you think. Trust in your ability to adapt and overcome obstacles. As J.K. Rowling said, "It’s our choices that show what we truly are, far more than our abilities."

Stay curious, open, and willing to take risks. The journey might be challenging, but it's also incredibly rewarding. Embrace uncertainty, and you will find strength and opportunities you never imagined.

Don't be afraid to ask for help. You will be surprised by the willingness of people who want to help you. Do not fight alone. Surround yourself with supportive people who encourage you to push your boundaries. Seek mentors who can offer guidance and perspective, and never stop investing in your personal growth. With the right mindset and support, you can handle any change and thrive in any situation.

So, embrace change, don't let fear dictate your choices, and live boldly. Your future self will thank you for it.

To the next generation of entrepreneurs, my advice is simple yet profound: only by adapting to change will you transform, both professionally and personally. Embrace the mantra "Adapt, Advance, Achieve," which is also the theme of my upcoming podcast.

Adaptation is key to thriving in an ever-changing world. Here's how you can embody ADAPT:

- **Acknowledge:** Recognise the need for change. Awareness is the first step towards transformation.
- **Define Goal:** Clearly articulate your objectives. Knowing what you want to achieve will guide your actions.
- **Assess:** Evaluate your current situation, resources, and challenges. Honest assessment prepares you effectively.
- **Plan:** Develop a strategy to reach your goals. Planning provides a roadmap and keeps you organised.
- **Transform:** Implement your plan and be ready to pivot. Transformation is continuous, and flexibility helps you navigate uncertainties.

Never stop learning. Continuous education and personal development are crucial for long-term success. The world evolves rapidly, and staying updated with new skills and trends will give you a competitive edge.

Remember, failing to adapt can be detrimental. Many companies, like Blockbuster, vanished because they couldn't evolve with the times.

The entrepreneurial journey is filled with highs and lows. Embrace each experience as an opportunity to learn and grow. Surround yourself with a supportive network, seek mentorship, and keep an open mind. By doing so, you'll not only achieve your goals but also inspire others to follow their dreams.

Stay curious, stay adaptable, and keep moving forward. Your future is shaped by the actions you take today.

Embracing change is essential for growth and success. Change can be intimidating, and the fear of the unknown can hold you back, but adapting to change unlocks your true potential.

In both personal and professional realms, being adaptable and flexible helps you navigate life's uncertainties. This mindset not only helps you overcome obstacles but also positions you to seize new opportunities.

By adopting the principles of "Adapt, Advance, Achieve," and embodying the acronym ADAPT—Acknowledge, Define Goal, Assess, Plan, and Transform—you can manage change effectively and turn challenges into opportunities. Continuous learning and personal development are vital components of this journey.

Do not let fear prevent you from living fully. Embrace change, learn from your experiences, and remain open to new possibilities. This approach will lead to personal and professional growth and help you build a resilient and fulfilling life. As Robin Sharma says, "All change is hard at first, messy in the middle, and gorgeous at the end."

About Me

As a wife, mother, and entrepreneur, I bring a vibrant legal career and a passion for connection to everything I do. Hailing from the multicultural island paradise of Mauritius, my fluency in French Creole and English reflects the rich tapestry of my heritage. My legal journey began in London, where I diligently built a successful career as a solicitor (England and Wales). This experience instilled in me a deep understanding of the intricacies of the UK legal system.

Returning to my roots in Mauritius, I embraced a new challenge, working for my family business. This experience honed my leadership skills and ignited my entrepreneurial spirit. Now, back in the UK since August 2022, I thrive on the synergy between my legal expertise and my diverse ventures.

I have established a thriving portfolio encompassing relocation and letting services, mediation, legal consultancy, and utilities brokerage for both residential and commercial clients. My unique background allows me to bridge the gap for Mauritians in the UK, providing them with specialised support for land succession and property transactions. I facilitate these processes by liaising with notaries in Mauritius to ensure all necessary documents are in order. My dedication to building strong client relationships and my fluency in English, French and Creole are invaluable assets in this niche area.

Two core values underpin my success: cultivating a robust network of mentors and collaborators and fostering a constant state of adaptability. These are the very principles I aim to share through my upcoming podcast, "Adapt, Advance, Achieve." In this project, I'll not only share my own experiences and hard-earned lessons, but also invite inspiring guests to share their stories and insights. Together, we'll empower listeners to navigate their own paths to success, equipping them with the tools and strategies to thrive in an ever-changing world.

Navigating Change

Suzette Metz
Employment Specialist
NHS Mental Health

"Change is the law of life. And those who look only to the past or present are certain to miss the future." – John F. Kennedy

My first encounter with change was at the age of six or seven years, in Jamaica living with my beloved grandmother. Yes, I was one of thousands of children left with grandparents, relatives, and friends to be raised or looked after while their parents went to, in my case, England to work.

My father left first, followed by mother maybe a year or so later. My dad was a trained electrician and my mother a seamstress. It took a long time for me to be aware of this change as I was a baby or toddler when they left. But as my consciousness grew, I realised they were missing and all I had of them were photographs that I cherished.

As I got a little older, it was notable very early that letters and barrels were only sent by my mother, and even at that young age I was aware there had been another change.

My grandmother was adorable and gave me complete unconditional love and I reciprocated. That said, I was always aware that my parents were not with us. There was a great sense of community in the small and impoverished place where we lived in Montego Bay, but for me there was always something missing. I spent many hours looking at a photo we had of my mum and dad, willing them to come to life.

As I got older and started school I came to terms with the change that occurred. There was regular contact, letters and barrels, filled with clothes and other things. I was always the best dressed in the yard! I went to school late as my grandmother couldn't afford to send me earlier, even though my mother did her best to support us. So, from the age of seven, I started going to school, another change. I struggled socially with the other children as I wasn't that used to mixing, a little over protectiveness from my grandmother. I did however learn very quickly to read and write. In no time I was able to send letters to my mum.

Another change had occurred: my mother was married to someone else, and I had two new siblings. More photos helped me to adjust to these changes. I now have siblings but felt very much as an only child. I had a few friends as I was attending school, which expanded my world a little. However, I still had a sense of being alone. I loved reading and remembered going to the library in Montego Bay most days after school. The library was on the beach, how cool is that? I have so many fond memories of walking home from the beach to have dinner with my grandmother.

Leaving Things Behind

Even at a young age, I had made some big adjustments as a result of change, and to a degree had accepted my life as it was in Jamaica with my grandmother, who I loved and adored. Then came the bombshell! Plans were afoot for me to move to England. There was an awareness that this was always the plan. But I couldn't leave my grandmother, she was sick and needed someone to care for, be with her and love her. This was a change, too far! I even sought advice from the few friends I had, who plotted with me regarding what I could do to avoid this fate. Some also envied me and wanted to go in my place.

There was real hardship where I lived in Jamaica at that time. It was the 60s and Jamaica had only been independent a few years. People, including me, sometimes experienced hunger. But despite that, I was now controlled by my emotions and did not want to leave the island and people I loved.

As well as my parents, my paternal grandmother and my maternal grandfather were also living and working in England. Hence the bureaucratic process to get me to England had started long before it came to my realisation. I remember at least two visits from my granddad; the both famous and infamous Mr Bono G (his nickname). Unbeknown to me he was quite a businessman. I remember him taking me to a pub that he owned and although I wasn't serving I was certainly working, doing the washing up. I loved it!

My granddad, however, was on a mission to get the motions in place for me to come to England. I was still having none of it. My friends were still suggesting ludicrous advice, ranging from destroying my clothes and passport to running away. Despite this, there were now firm plans in place for me to leave Jamaica.

This change was huge for me at the age of seven. Even at that age I knew that not only did I love my grandmother deeply and did not want to leave, I loved Jamaica and did not want to leave her either. Change is an interesting phenomenon. I struggled with the change of not having my parents at a very young age, and pined for them, but I also didn't want to change the life that I was experiencing as an older child. I used to walk along the beach after leaving the library wondering what my life would be like if I was not able to walk on my beautiful beach and hug and love my grandmother.

I eventually left my beloved gran and Jamaica in 1968. I remember the journey on a BOAC aeroplane, on my own, cared for on my journey by a kind air hostess and made a friend on my 12 hour journey with a stop off in America. She was older than me and nice. I wished I had had the sense to take her details. I didn't see her after I arrived at Heathrow Airport. Awaiting me was my mum, dad and youngest sister in my new family. More change. I remember the drive to my new home and looking out of the car window on that August day which was mildly sunny, but appeared bleak to me. There was little or no sunshine, just grey buildings. I laid down in the car and cried.

New Responsibilities

I was now the eldest sister of four other children at nearly nine years old. Being the eldest sibling came with lots of responsibilities. There were so many adjustments to make meeting your mother, father, stepfather, stepmother, siblings and wider family members on my father's side were overwhelming and difficult to adjust to at first. However, even at a young age it was dawning on me that change was an inevitable part of life and something to embrace not to run away from.

Starting school was a joy as I love learning. Sadly, like most people of colour, I faced racism at school from the teachers as well as the children. My teachers were surprised at how well I could read. My mother had done a good job at preparing me for the racism that I might experience at school and in the wider community, as most West Indian parents gave their children the talk. This basically explained that, particularly at school, we had to always work harder to prove we were just as good. Hence, I was well prepared for this change even though it is never a change that was acceptable to me.

I think it is fair to say that as I grew into adulthood, I embraced change more and more, and fast forward a few decades, I was introduced to a book by Dr. Spencer Johnson called, Who Moved My Cheese. This book left a lasting impression on me, and I went on to read a few of his books in a series about change. Cheese being a metaphor for what is wanted in life, for example loving relationships, a nice job, abundance of money, possessions, good health, spirituality, and peace of mind. Mice seek their cheese in a maze, this could also be family, community or workplace. Big problem is our cheese keeps moving, same as in the story of the mice in the maze whose cheese is constantly being moved. One of them deals with this constant change successfully and shares his discovery by writing on the walls of the maze what he had learned, for others to discover.

I would like to think that I accept that change will always happen and that we can learn from change and grow from it. It is something I have tried to share and support others through both in my personal and professional life. I currently work as a health care professional supporting people with mental health difficulties and in their recovery. Particularly people with severe mental health difficulties who often lose their livelihood, their homes, and sometimes their families and need tangible, and emotional support to rebuild their lives.

I remember many years ago speaking to a very senior healthcare professional in the NHS who had a diagnosis of bipolar. He explained that when he was well and in charge of a department with hundreds of people, he was capable of making numerous decisions daily, but when he was unwell he was not able to decide which colour socks to buy in a shop. Now, that is what you call change. Although change for the most part is good, some changes require support to get through.

I have had the privilege, over the past 30 or so years, to support people with disabilities and help them to adjust to the changes they have experienced because of their disability or long-term health conditions.

A mental illness causes changes in the brain of individuals in the way they are able to think, feel, and act. Mood changes include feeling sad and more worried. Being newly diagnosed with a mental health difficulty leads to life altering changes in various ways. This includes being affected emotionally, socially and financially impacting on lifestyle, employment, education, self esteem and identity. This in turn can affect long term planning and coping strategies.

Emotional Impact: An individual may have a sense of relief to have an explanation for their experiences. Others may experience fear or anxiety about their diagnosis and its implication. Concerns about stigma and changes to their self perception.

Adjustments to Lifestyle: This change requires adjustments to daily routines (such as taking medication daily and monitoring for side effects), regular therapy and changes in diet, sleep, exercise and stress management.

Socially: Changes to social interactions; decisions about whom to disclose to and inform about diagnosis and managing their reactions. Changes to social interactions, and activities based on new limitations and recommendations by health care professionals.

Financial: Cost associated with medication, therapy and other treatment and insurance cover for insurance premiums for mental health cover.

Employment and Education: Disclosure of a mental health condition to an employer is a major change to anyone's life as this could lead to stigma. Adjustments at work, and in colleges and school are usually required.

Self Esteem and Identity: Integrating a sense of self and understanding what it means to your identity and self esteem related to a diagnosis is a massive change to anyone.

Long-Term Planning: Changes to future plans and a re-evaluation of life's goals based on a new diagnosis is common. Working with health care professionals to provide treatment and care plans.

Developing New Coping Strategies: Learning new strategies such as mindfulness and relaxation techniques, meditation and exercises have all helped individuals to cope with a diagnosis.

These changes are challenging, but with support from family, friends and health professionals, most people can successfully adapt and find ways to lead fulfilling lives.

Mental Health And Change

It is important when working with people who experience mental health difficulties to give them hope, and I would often do this by talking about other people who have managed to adjust to this change. Most people are able to relate to famous people in the public eye, who have made this adjustment to change.

So many people's lives have changed after a mental health diagnosis, here are a few examples; Glen Close, the famous actress, has spoken about her family's experience of mental ill health. Her sister has a diagnosis of bipolar disorder, and her nephew has a diagnosis of schizoaffective disorder. This diagnosis has led her to co-found Bring Change to Mind, an organisation aimed at combating the stigma surrounding mental ill health. Catherine Zeta-Jones revealed publicly her diagnosis.

In 2011, she raised awareness about the illness with her openness and encouraged people to seek help. Other notable, famous British people have openly discussed their mental health diagnosis; Stephen Fry diagnosed with bipolar, Prince Harry, Duke of Sussex who struggled with post traumatic stress and anxiety and with anxiety in particular following the death of his mother Princess Diana, who also struggled with severe depression, bulimia, and self harm. She also brought significant attention to the issues around mental health. Emma Thompson, acclaimed actress and screenwriter, has also spoken openly about her battle with depression. Alistair Campbell who was the last Labour Party's political strategist and writer has been very candid about his experience with depression and alcoholism. Zayn Malik, former member of

One Direction has opened up about his struggles with anxiety which has led him to cancel performances.

These famous individuals' struggles with mental health highlight the impact a diagnosis can have, not only on personal wellbeing and stability, but also in their contributions to mental health advocacy and reducing stigma. They have used their platforms to share their struggles and the changes that mental health has had on their lives to promote understanding and support.

Change can have profound impacts on us all whether we have good mental health or bad mental health. On a personal level it can lead to growth, pushing individuals out of their comfort zone, allowing new skills and perspectives to develop, and as already discussed; can cause stress and anxiety and poor mental health. On a positive note, regular exposure to change can improve adaptability and resilience, which can make future changes easier to handle.

Change can also drive innovation and lead to improvements of processes, services and products in organisations. Change delivered well can boost employees morale. Therefore, effective management of change in organisations is key as poorly managed change can lead to resistance and dissatisfaction. Hence, organisations that adapt well to change can gain or maintain a competitive edge in their industry.

Changes in society can lead to progress in equality, justice and public health. Positive changes in markets, policies, and technology can impact our economy, affecting employment and wealth distribution. Cultural changes can alter social values and behaviours which, over time, shape societal identity. Economic and global changes in trade policies can affect opportunities, local economies, and international trade.

It is always good to have strategies to manage change. Good and effective communication can alleviate fears around change and reduce resistance. Seeking effective support and resources is also important. For example, training, counselling and therapy are all interventions that can help individuals cope with change. Effective leadership, peer support and family support can help with the transition through change particularly for mental ill health.

Many people with a diagnosis of severe mental ill health do not work, and a high proportion once diagnosed lose their jobs if they are employed as a result of long periods of being off work and receiving treatment from mental health services. They then often become long term service users, if there is no intervention such as from an NHS employment practitioner, like myself, who are able to contact employers with the view to retaining the service user's job.

Understanding the impact of change and employing strategies,such as a wellbeing in work plan to manage it effectively, can help individuals and organisations to navigate transitions smoothly and capitalise on new opportunities.

Therefore, I have supported people to manage change with their mental health diagnosis who are in work, which involves creating an accommodating, supportive, and empathic environment with personalised plans based on the individual's specific needs and diagnosis. It is vital to involve the employee in creating this plan in order to ensure it meets their needs effectively. Any changes must always be communicated in advance to the person whenever possible, using communication methods that the individual will understand.

I have used unique models of recovery support particularly for people with mental health diagnosis gain and sustain employment. Helping them to mitigate the changes required to navigate the world of work after a mental health diagnosis. Helping them to identify the benefits of change. There is always a built in resistance to change, as a practitioner it is my job to sell the benefits of change by working, but they also need to see the benefits of change for themself. Pros and cons exercises are good to imply when supporting a client through change. However, the reason for change must always come from the individual and their motivation to work.

My role as a recovery practitioner who supports people with disabilities and mental ill health is to gain and sustain employment. The roles I have had have required me to specialise in helping individuals to overcome their barriers to employment and gain confidence as inclusive members of society. What I have not mentioned is the emotional support that is required when helping someone with a physical or mental health condition to adjust to a massive change in their lives.

I remember someone several years ago who had lost his job,and was well enough to start applying for work again after his diagnosis. The application process can be gruelling; not being shortlisted for interviews after completing application form after application form. This client broke down in tears. He didn't want to apply for any more jobs and didn't believe he could do it. At that point I reminded him that he was not alone in the process and that I was there to help, even when he no longer believed. I had to hold the belief that he could get a job. Eventually, he did go on to get a job in the charity sector and is still working now with some added adjustments.

I am a recovery mental health practitioner, coach, and mentor with over thirty years experience working in job centres, the National Health Service and other organisations providing support, and helping others adjusting to change that will benefit social inclusivity. I am committed to help and support people who are marginalised and disadvantaged to identify their goals and grow in their chosen professions regardless of the changes that occur in their lives. In doing so, I have helped numerous individuals move from unemployment to employment or self-employment.

I am all about changing lives and seeing the positive impact.

About Me

I am a dedicated specialist employment worker with a strong commitment to assisting individuals diagnosed with long-term health conditions, especially individuals diagnosed with mental health conditions. Over many years, I have played a pivotal role in helping numerous clients overcome barriers to employment, fostering their professional and personal growth. My empathetic and solution oriented approach has empowered many to achieve stability and success in the workplace.

In addition to my professional achievements, I am a proud mother of two young adults. Balancing my career with motherhood, I have instilled in my children, values of resilience, compassion, and perseverance. My role as a mother deeply informs my work (as one of my children has a learning difficulty), ethics and dedication to creating supportive and nurturing environments both at home and in my professional life.

Beyond my primary role, I serve as a mentor and coach, guiding individuals through personal and career challenges. My mentorship is marked by a deep understanding of the complexities surrounding mental health and employment allowing me to provide tailored advice and support. My coaching style is compassionate yet motivating, encouraging my mentees to reach their full potential.

My unwavering dedication to helping others, combined with my practical expertise and nurturing nature, has made a significant impact on the lives of many, both within my professional sphere and beyond.

Conclusion

In the end, change is unavoidable. Yet, through every challenge, it moulds us into our present selves and will continue shaping who we are destined to be.

As you navigate the changes in your own life, let these lessons guide you to adapt boldly towards the transformation that is about to take place.

- Change often starts with discomfort as it disrupts familiarity and invites us to explore new ways of thinking and doing
- Change teaches us to adapt our plans and expectations as circumstances evolve
- Change requires courage, and often involves facing uncertainties with bravery
- Change sparks creativity as we search for solutions in unfamiliar territory
- Change invites reflection as it pushes us to evaluate our values, goals, and priorities

- Change brings opportunities amid uncertainty, it opens doors to new possibilities and experiences

Some changes are beyond your control, while others can be made entirely by yourself. Regardless of the type of change you encounter, each offers valuable lessons and the potential to lead you towards a life of extraordinary possibilities, far beyond what your current self can envision.

Allow yourself to cry about change, laugh about change, talk openly about change, but ultimately... embrace it wholeheartedly and see where it takes you.

Printed in Great Britain
by Amazon

46502330R00126